To Saomaï and Bà,

To my ancestors,

To my family,

To the future generations,

"Food is one of the strongest ties many emigrants have with their ancestral past."
— Andrée Chedid, *The Multiple Child*

TASTING VIETNAM

FLAVORS AND MEMORIES
FROM MY GRANDMOTHER'S KITCHEN

ANNE-SOLENNE HATTE,

FROM THE RECIPE COLLECTIONS OF BÀ NGOẠI

Rizzoli NEW YORK

New York · Paris · London · Milan

Here is a book that takes us on a journey. Traveling through space and time, Anne-Solenne tells the story of Bà, her grandmother, beginning in the 1920s in Hanoi, Hué, and later Saigon. We follow her into exile, first to Washington, D.C., and then to France. She arrives in Blois, in the Loire Valley, in the 1960s, then finally settles in Orléans. Most of all, this book is an exploration of emotions. The great Alain Chapel used to say that "cooking is much more than recipes"; this book gives very moving evidence of that principle, ranging from solemn and serious—war, loss, and exile—to sweet and tender, as manifested in Anne-Solenne's attachment to Bà. Emotion links them both to the memory of their ancestors' country, Vietnam, and to their love of their adopted country, France.

And where is the food in all of this? It is at the heart of the story. Each recipe evokes a family anecdote and the tastes that are indelibly associated with it. The dishes are light and healthful, often plant-based. The cuisine is aromatic and flavorful, deriving a great deal of subtlety from cilantro, lemongrass, sesame, ginger, and tia to. It is a cuisine with that innate elegance, which only the world's great culinary traditions are able to display in everyday cooking.

We must thank Anne-Solenne Hatte for her immense generosity. Indeed, with this book, she gives us two gifts. The first gift is that of delicious and exotic recipes, collected from Bà and described with great talent. And she offers us a gift of even greater value: a message of courage, peace, and love. And isn't that, in the end, the entire point of cooking?

Alain Ducasse

I would like to tell you the story of Bà, my grandmother.

It is the story of a woman and her journey from the world of rice paddies in Vietnam to the White House. She lived in Orléans in France. She had nine children, fifteen grandchildren, and twelve great-grandchildren. Standing only four feet seven inches (140 centimeters) tall and married to President Diem's right-hand man, my grandfather, she was a woman like no other.

Her story is a story we can all identify with, because it is a love story. It is a tribute to all the families who fled the Vietnam War, immigrating to the United States, Canada, or France to rebuild their lives.

The dishes Bà prepared allowed her to preserve her family. Her rice porridge helped them to survive the Great Famine; her duck breast with bamboo shoots won the hearts of Americans during the war; and later her restaurant in France, La Hanoïenne, permitted her to pay for the studies of her nine children and draw the attention of the *Gault and Millau* restaurant guide.

I am therefore a "grandchild of war."

Had it not been for that conflict, I never would have been born. I am Eurasian, with a French father and a Vietnamese mother. To be Eurasian is to accept one's own complementarity. My grandmother's recipes for traditional Vietnamese dishes—which you will find throughout the pages of this book—form the core of my cultural heritage today. It is something that I, in turn, would like to pass on to my children and grandchildren.

Memory is a treasure. Paying homage to it is another; it is also a source of strength. I would like to put this silence, these absences, into words to understand where I come from to better understand who I am. I would like to share this both painful and uplifting story, because, despite the heartbreak my family has experienced, it remains an example of determination, love, and happiness. This is the reason I would like, through this book, to give Bà the opportunity to speak.

My grandmother's story is the account of an indomitable woman who brought her memories to life through timeless flavors. This journey is her story. And her recipes are now immortal.

Anne-Solenne

"Tell me where you come from, Bà, and I'll tell you who I am."
Anne-Solenne

Contents

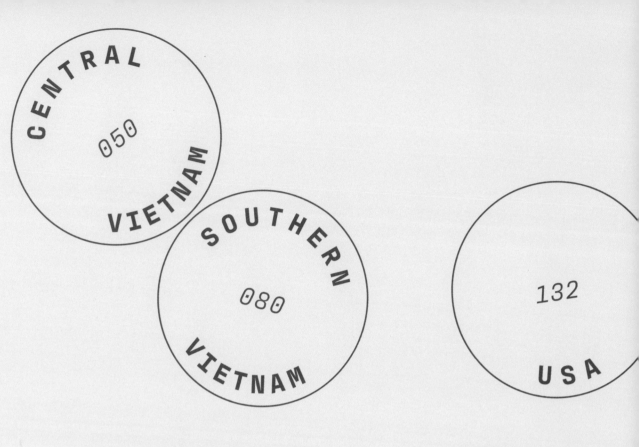

NORTHERN VIETNAM

I come from a very small village called Vân Nội, just under seven miles
(eleven kilometers) from the city of Hanoi. Today, the village has become a part of the city.

My father was a rice farmer. He was thin but very strong. My mother was
beautiful and sweet, but there was sadness in her face.
She was so unhappy that it led to her death. They were
parents of three children. I am the eldest sibling. I
became a mother before my time, because I had to take
care of my two little brothers after our mother died. The
youngest was one month old. I was ten years old.
I remember the rice paddies around the house, the warmth of the sun
caressing the growing shoots.

My fondest childhood memory is being with my father. In the morning,
he would take me out to eat phở. I loved getting on his
shoulders and crossing the large mud puddle in front of
the house. He was my hero, and I was his princess.

The word *phở* is derived from *pot-au-feu*, the French beef stew. This Tonkinese noodle soup was created after the French arrived. In fact, we could have called it *pot-au-phở* as a reference to the French.

Phở bò

Broth base

1¼ pounds (600 g) beef short ribs

10½ ounces (300 g) marrow bones

10½ ounces (300 g) oxtail

1¼ pounds (600 g) beef tenderloin

1 tablespoon (20 g) salt

1 (2-inch/5-cm) piece fresh ginger (80 g)

2 white onions (7 ounces/200 g)

1½ pounds (700 g) white turnips

3 whole star anise

1½ tablespoons (8 g) black cardamom pods

1 teaspoon (2 g) green cardamom pods

1 (¼-ounce/8-g) cinnamon stick

1 tablespoon (5 g) coriander seeds

2 tablespoons (30 g) nuoc mam (fish sauce)

3½ tablespoons (40 g) sugar (optional)

Noodles

1 teaspoon (6 g) salt

2 (14-ounce/400-g) packages Bun phô rice vermicelli noodles

Accompaniments

Herbs: scallions, cilantro leaves, Thai basil, ngo gai (culantro)

1 white onion (3½ ounces/100 g)

3 tablespoons rice vinegar

2 limes

Freshly ground black pepper

2 fresh Thai chiles (6 g; optional)

Preparation time:
30 minutes
Cooking time: 5 hours

TIPS
• If you do not have a
gas burner, lightly toast
the ginger and onion in
a preheated 475°F (250°C)
oven for 5 minutes.

FOR THE BROTH BASE

— Fill a stockpot with 5 quarts plus
1 cup (5 liters) water and bring to a boil over high heat. Add the
ribs, marrow bones, and oxtail and blanch for 15 to 20 minutes. Set
aside the raw tenderloin. About 5 minutes after the scum appears,
take everything out of the pot and discard the cooking water. Rinse
the meat to remove any impurities. Fill the pot with 5 quarts plus
1 cup (5 liters) cold water and add the 1 tablespoon (20 g) salt.
Return the meat to the pot and place over high heat. When the
broth comes to a boil, reduce the heat to low and cook for about
1 hour 30 minutes, skimming regularly.

Peel the ginger, spear with a fork, and char over a flame for
5 minutes on each side. Use a mortar and pestle to crush the ginger.
Peel the onions and char the outer layer of each over a flame. Peel
and cut the turnips into 1¼-inch (3-cm) chunks. Add the ginger,
charred onion, and turnips to the broth • .

In a small skillet over low heat, toast the star anise, black cardamom, green cardamom, cinnamon stick, and coriander seeds for about
5 minutes, stirring constantly. As soon as the aromas are released,
remove from the heat and use a mortar and pestle to crush the spices.
Tie in a cheesecloth bag and add to the broth. Add the nuoc mam and,
if needed, adjust the flavor with the sugar. Continue to cook for an additional 1 hour, or until the meat is very soft. Remove the meat to a plate
and let cool. Reduce the heat and simmer the broth for another 1 hour.

FOR THE NOODLES

— Fill a large saucepan with 10½ cups
(2.5 liters) water. Add the salt, and bring to a boil over high heat.
Add the rice noodles and cook for 10 minutes. Drain, rinse in cold
water, and set aside.

FOR THE ACCOMPANIMENTS

— Wash the herbs. Chop the scallions and cilantro leaves. Peel the onion, slice it into thin rings, and put into a bowl. Stir in the vinegar. Quarter the limes lengthwise. Finally, cut the raw beef tenderloin and cooled rib meat into very thin slices. Set aside separately •• .

•• The cilantro stems can be added to the broth for extra flavor. Remove before serving.

ASSEMBLY AND SERVING

— Remove the spice bag from the pot and strain the broth. Return the broth to the pot and bring to a boil. Put 1 cup (200 g) rice noodles into each serving bowl. Add five or six slices of cooked meat and pour a ladle of hot soup into each bowl to warm for 30 seconds. Transfer the broth in the bowl back into the pot and bring back to a boil. Add five or six slices of raw meat to each bowl, together with the herbs and a sprinkling of freshly ground pepper. Pour in a ladle of hot broth.

Serve the bowls of hot phở bò with the pickled onions and a lime wedge. Add a little chile, if desired ••• .

Enjoy the delicious flavor!

••• You can add sliced chile or a few drops of sriracha (chile sauce).

In southern Vietnam, a spoonful of hoisin sauce is added for its sweetness.

Do not discard the oxtail; shred the meat and save it for another dish, use it as an accompaniment for predinner drinks, or serve it in the broth with the rest of the meat.

When I was sixteen years old, I entered a beauty contest. My hair was so long that it reached my ankles. I impressed everyone and won the prize!
As a result, I received nineteen marriage proposals. My father was furious, because I turned them all down.

You know, what mattered to me was freedom!

Bún chả

Preparation time: 1 hour
Cooking time: 30 minutes
Resting time: 30 minutes

TIPS
• To enhance the flavor
of this dish, you can add
4 teaspoons (20 g) rice
wine to the marinade. The
marinade is even better
when made the previous
day or at least six hours
before cooking.

•• Never store meat
in its package in the
refrigerator; allow it to
have contact with the air
inside. The same goes for
fish.

— Fill a large saucepan with 4¼ cups
(1 liter) cold water. Add the noodles and a pinch of salt, and bring to a boil
over medium heat. Cook for 5 to 10 minutes. Turn off the heat, cover, and
let stand for 5 minutes. Drain, rinse in cold water, and set aside.

— Prepare the marinade: Peel the shal-
lots and garlic. Mince the shallots, garlic, and lemongrass. Combine in
a bowl and add the nuoc mam, sugar, 3 tablespoons (40 g) sunflower
oil, and pepper •.

— Pat the meat dry with paper towels,
remove the layer of fat ••, and cut into slices. Marinate in the refrigerator for at least 3 hours. Divide and thread onto four skewers, leaving
some space between each slice. Heat some sunflower oil in a skillet over medium heat and cook for about 30 minutes, turning every
5 minutes. Alternatively, cook them directly on a grill.
    Accompany the skewers with the noodles, lettuce, tia to, mint,
sliced cucumbers, pickled carrots, pickled onions, and cilantro. Serve
with the spring roll dipping sauce.

Pork and marinade

3 to 5 shallots (80 g)

4 cloves garlic (12 g)

1 (3-ounce/80-g) stalk lemongrass

5 tablespoons plus 1 teaspoon (80 g) nuoc mam (fish sauce)

¼ cup (50 g) sugar

3 tablespoons (40 g) sunflower oil, plus more as needed

½ teaspoon (1.25 g) ground black pepper

1¼ pounds (600 g) pork belly (not too fatty)

Accompaniments

7 ounces (200 g) rice vermicelli noodles

Salt

16 butter lettuce leaves

12 tia to (Vietnamese perilla) leaves

12 fresh mint leaves

¾ cup (80 g) sliced cucumber

⅔ cup (100 g) pickled carrots (page 85, Tip)

⅔ cup (100 g) pickled onions (page 122)

16 sprigs cilantro

Spring Roll Dipping Sauce (page 211)

Bánh cuốn
nhân thịt lợn

Preparation time:
50 minutes
Cooking time: 30 minutes
Resting time: 1 hour

FOR THE PANCAKE BATTER

— Combine the rice flour and salt in a bowl. Mix with 3⅓ cups (0.8 liter) water, cover with plastic wrap, and rest for 1 hour.

Remove the excess water by tilting the bowl slightly over the sink. Heat 4¼ cups (1 liter) water to about 120°F (50°C) and pour it into the dough from a height while mixing it.

FOR THE FILLING

— Soak the wood ear mushrooms in a bowl filled with warm water for 15 minutes, then remove and cut into small dice. Peel and thinly slice the onions. Heat the sunflower oil in a large skillet over medium heat and brown the onions. Add the mushrooms and brown, then add the meat and brown. Season with the nuoc mam and pepper, reduce the heat, cover, and cook for 10 minutes, stirring occasionally. Remove from the heat and set aside.

COOKING AND ASSEMBLY

— Add 1½ tablespoons (20 g) of the reserved shallot frying oil to the bánh cuôn pancake batter. Heat a small crepe pan until very hot •. Add a little of the shallot frying oil, followed by a small ladle of batter spread to cover the entire surface of the pan. Remove any excess batter. Cover with a lid and cook for 30 seconds, then transfer the pancake to an oiled plate. Use a small spoon to put a ¾-ounce (20-g) mound of filling in the center of the pancake and fold four sides over to cover the filling. Set aside. Repeat the process to make 20 bánh cuôn.

Garnish with cilantro and fried shallots and accompany with your choice of dipping sauce.

Pancake batter

3¾ cups (500 g) rice flour

1 teaspoon (5 g) salt

Filling

3¼ ounces (90 g) wood ear mushrooms

2 to 3 small onions (6½ ounces/180 g)

2 tablespoons (30 g) sunflower oil

6½ ounces (180 g) ground pork shoulder

1 tablespoon (14 g) nuoc mam (fish sauce)

¼ teaspoon (1.5 g) ground black pepper

1 recipe (5½ ounces/160 g) Fried Shallots and cooking oil (page 212)

Finishing

Cilantro

Bánh Cuốn Dipping Sauce (page 212) or Spring Roll Dipping Sauce (page 211) • •

SERVES 4

Pancake batter

3¾ cups (500 g) rice flour

1 teaspoon (5 g) salt

1 recipe (5½ ounces/160 g) Fried Shallots and cooking oil (page 212)

Filling

2¼ ounces (60 g) wood ear mushrooms

1 onion (3½ ounces/100 g)

4 scallions

7 ounces (200 g) head- and shell-on large shrimp

2 tablespoons (30 g) sunflower oil

2½ teaspoons (12 g) nuoc mam (fish sauce)

Freshly ground black pepper

Finishing

Shrimp Bisque (page 212)

Cilantro

Bánh cuốn tôm

NORTHERN VIETNAM

Preparation time: 1 hour
Cooking time: 30 minutes
Resting time: Overnight

FOR THE PANCAKE BATTER

— Make the bánh cuốn pancake batter following the directions for Bánh Cuôn with Pork (page 22), starting a day ahead. Prepare the fried shallots following the directions (page 212) and set aside, along with the frying oil.

FOR THE FILLING

— Soak the wood ear mushrooms in a bowl filled with warm water for 15 minutes, then remove and cut into small dice. Peel and thinly slice the onions. Mince the scallions.

Peel and devein the shrimp (make a shallow slit along the back and remove the black intestine) and remove the heads. Cut the shrimp into small cubes. Reserve the heads and shells to make the bisque.

Heat the sunflower oil in a large skillet over medium heat and brown the onions. Add the mushrooms and brown. Add the shrimp and nuoc mam, increase the heat to high, and sear for 1 minute, or until just cooked through. Add the scallion and season with pepper.

COOKING AND ASSEMBLY

— Make a bisque with the reserved shrimp heads and shells (page 212).

Cook the pancakes and assemble the bánh cuôn in exactly the same way as for the Bánh Cuôn with Pork • . Accompany with the bisque and garnish with cilantro and fried shallots •• .

TIPS
• Add a tablespoon of shallot oil in the batter before cooking.
The pan must be very hot when making the pancakes.
•• You may add a dash of lime juice or finger lime pearls.

Back in 1936, Dang was my best friend. He was younger than me, but he was spirited and full of life, which left an impression on me. He was already a soldier at heart. He had always been in love with me, but being a Buddhist, he couldn't marry me.

In 1945, at the end of World War II, we experienced a very serious food shortage, known as the Great Famine or "the famine of the year At Dau" in French Indochina. It killed a million people in North Vietnam while the country was under Japanese occupation. Dang asked me to help him and to join his movement. So every day I would prepare a huge pot of rice porridge to feed orphaned children.

Rice porridge is the cheapest and most nutritious soup. A single handful of rice grains can feed four people. It is called *cháo* in Vietnamese.

Cháo

Preparation time: 30 minutes
Cooking time: 1 hour

— Wash both types of rice together three times in warm water.

Pour 4 quarts plus 1 cup (4 liters) cold water into a saucepan and add the rice and salt. Cook over medium heat for 45 minutes, stirring regularly to prevent the rice from sticking to the bottom of the pan and reducing the heat for the final 15 minutes. The rice is done when it appears soft and translucent. Turn off the heat and cover the pan with a lid to keep it warm.

— Chop the beef into small pieces. Peel and finely dice the shallots. Wash and mince the herbs. Set aside.

— Put one ladle of rice porridge into a bowl. Arrange the chopped beef in the center with a little diced shallot and herbs. Season with a sprinkling of pepper •. Adjust the seasoning with a little nuoc mam, if necessary ••.

TIPS
• If you prefer the meat to cook more, put it into the bowl before adding the rice porridge.
•• This dish can be served with ruôc (pork floss; page 32), chicken, or tripe, or simply with herbs.

SERVES
4

1 cup (160 g) white rice

¼ cup (40 g) glutinous (sticky)
rice

2 teaspoons (10 g) salt

7 ounces (200 g) beef tenderloin

2 to 4 shallots (60 g)

Herbs: cilantro leaves, scallions,
rau ram (Vietnamese cilantro)

Freshly ground black pepper

Nuoc mam (fish sauce),
if needed

Preparation time for
the three different xôi:
30 minutes

Yellow Xôi
Cooking time: 1 hour
Resting time:
4 hours 30 minutes

Red Xôi
Cooking time: 30 minutes
Resting time:
4 hours 20 minutes

Peanut Xôi
Cooking time: 30 minutes
Resting time: Overnight
plus 4 hours 30 minutes

TIP
• *Traditional recipes*
use melted lard instead
of coconut liquid.

FOR THE XÔI BASE

— Wash the rice three times, then soak in a bowl of warm water for 4 hours. Transfer to a strainer and drain for 20 minutes.

FOR THE YELLOW XÔI

— Rinse the mung beans, then soak in a bowl of warm water for 4 hours.

Drain the mung beans, being careful to remove any impurities and traces of skin still adhering to the beans. Put into a steamer with water. As soon as the steam rises, cover with the lid and steam for 30 minutes. Remove from the heat, transfer the beans to a bowl, and let cool for 5 to 10 minutes. Sprinkle with 2½ teaspoons (15 g) salt and gently mix with chopsticks. Use a mortar and pestle to grind the beans to a smooth paste. Put the rice into a bowl and crumble the bean paste over the top. Mix well to completely incorporate. Add the remaining 1½ teaspoons (10 g) salt and gently mix with chopsticks, then put everything into the steamer. When the steam rises, steam for 30 minutes. Put the shredded coconut into a bowl with 1 cup plus 1 tablespoon (250 ml) water and soak for 20 minutes. Strain the coconut liquid and discard the pulp. Remove the rice and bean mixture from the steamer, add the coconut liquid, and mix gently •. Serve.

FOR THE RED XÔI

— Season the drained rice with the salt. Remove the flesh from around the gac fruit seeds and carefully mix with the rice, making sure the rice does not become compacted. Heat water in a steamer. As soon as the steam rises, put the mixture into the steamer basket and steam for 30 minutes. After about 15 minutes, when halfway cooked, gently stir the rice grains. Put the shredded coconut into a bowl with 1 cup plus 1 tablespoon (250 ml) water and soak for 20 minutes. Strain the coconut liquid and discard the pulp. Pour over the cooked rice, then add the sugar and rice wine. Return to the steamer for 5 minutes. If you want, decorate the top of the xôi with the gac fruit seeds when serving.

FOR THE PEANUT XÔI

A day ahead, soak the peanuts in water overnight.

— Season the drained rice with the salt. Drain the peanuts and carefully mix them with the rice. Heat water in a steamer. As soon as the steam rises, put the mixture into the steamer basket and steam for 30 minutes. After about 15 minutes, when halfway cooked, tap on the sides of the steamer basket to mix the rice grains.

Enjoy this xôi as they do in the south with sugar and fried shallots (page 212) or as they do in the north with nuoc mam.

Xôi

NORTHERN VIETNAM

SERVES 4

Xôi base

2¾ cups (500 g) glutinous
(sticky) rice

Yellow xôi

1 cup (200 g) dried mung beans

4 teaspoons (25 g) salt

2 cups (150 g) shredded dried
coconut

Red xôi

2½ teaspoons (15 g) salt

9 ounces (250 g) gac fruit

2 cups (150 g) shredded dried
coconut

2 tablespoons (25 g) sugar

2 tablespoons (35 g) rice wine

Peanut xôi

2 cups (300 g) raw peanuts,
shelled with skins on

2½ teaspoons (15 g) salt

When cooked, this meat has a fluffy texture resembling raw cotton. This is why it is also called thịt chà bông, which means "pork shredded like cotton." As children, we would say that this dish looked like wool.

Ruốc

12½ ounces (350 g) pork tenderloin

1 shallot (20 g)

2 teaspoons (10 g) sunflower oil

1½ tablespoons (20 g) sugar

3 tablespoons plus 1 teaspoon (50 g) nuoc mam (fish sauce)

Preparation time: 30 minutes
Cooking time: 40 minutes to 1 hour
Resting time: 1 to 2 hours

— Carefully remove any fat from the meat. Cut into 3¼-inch (8-cm) chunks.

Peel and mince the shallot. Heat the sunflower oil in a large saucepan over medium heat and sweat the shallot. Add the meat, ⅔ cup (150 g) water, the sugar, and nuoc mam. Turn the meat over, cover with a lid, and cook for 15 minutes. As soon as the water comes to a simmer, reduce the heat and carefully turn over the meat to preserve its texture. Cook for 30 minutes. The meat is cooked when it is dry and firm to the touch. Let cool, then refrigerate for 1 to 2 hours.

— Use a mortar and pestle to crush one piece of meat at a time without damaging the fibers. Use your hands to shred the meat, separating the fibers while keeping them soft and moist. Put the shredded meat into a skillet over low heat and cook for 5 to 10 minutes, carefully stirring regularly. The pork floss is ready when it has dried out further and become even softer, with the appearance of raw cotton. Transfer to a dish and let cool.

— This meat can be eaten with white rice or rice porridge (page 28), or simply on lightly buttered bread • .

TIP
• *The meat will keep for up to one week.*
The same recipe can be made using fresh ham, fish, and chicken.

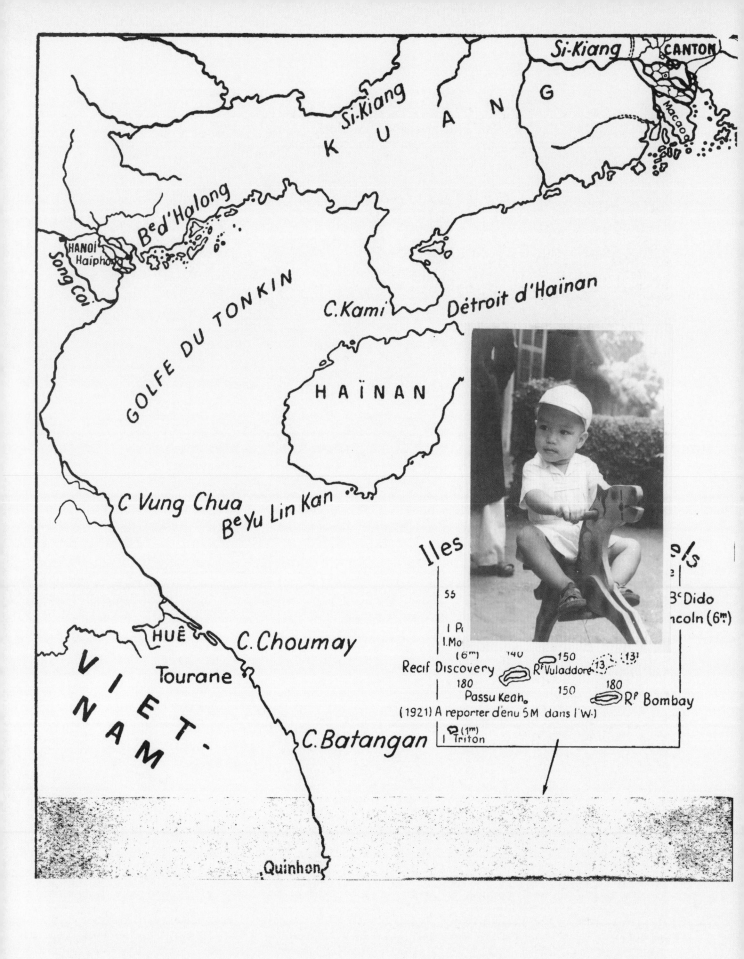

Si-Kiang CANTON

Macao

KUANG

Si-Kiang

B ᵉ d'Halong

HANOÏ
Haiphong

Song Coi

GOLFE DU TONKIN

C. Kami Détroit d'Haïnan

HAÏNAN

C Vung Chua
Bᵉ Yu Lin Kan

Iles

55

1 P
1. Mo
(6ᵐ)   140   150   13   13
Recif Discovery   Rᶠ Vuladdore
         180   150   180
      Passu Keah   Rᶠ Bombay
(1921) A reporter d'enu 5M dans l'W·)

Bᶜ Dido
ncoln (6ᵐ)

HUÊ C. Choumay

Tourane

VIET.

NAM

C. Batangan

🐚 (1ᵐ)
1 Triton

Quinhon

Later on, the Indochina War made things more difficult. It was not only necessary to feed the children but also the Vietnamese soldiers who had gone to the front line to fight the French.

Dang's younger sister came to help me. We had become so close that she ended up taking the same name as me. Dang, however, devoted himself body and soul to fighting for the cause, despite his young age. He was only sixteen years old and was the youngest soldier to enlist. I saw him less and less, and I was worried about him.

Bánh tôm

Serves 4

Preparation time: 30 minutes
Cooking time: 10 minutes
Resting time: 30 minutes

2 (2½-inch/6.5-cm) pieces fresh turmeric (30 g)

¾ cup plus 1 tablespoon (100 g) pastry flour

⅓ cup (50 g) rice flour

1 egg

½ teaspoon (3 g) plus 1 pinch salt

1 to 2 sweet potatoes (7 ounces/200 g)

2½ ounces (70 g) large raw shrimp (with thin shells)

2 cups (400 g) sunflower oil

Butter lettuce, for serving

Herbs: cilantro, mint

1 small bowl filled with Spring Roll Dipping Sauce (page 211)

— Start by making the batter. Peel the turmeric. Use a mortar and pestle to grind it with 1 teaspoon (5 g) water. Strain the juice obtained and set aside. Combine the pastry flour, 2 teaspoons (10 g) water, the rice flour, egg, and ½ teaspoon (2 g) of the salt in a bowl. Mix to incorporate, then add the turmeric juice and mix again. Let rest for 30 minutes.

— Peel and cut the sweet potatoes into matchsticks. Season the shrimp with a pinch of salt. Set everything aside.

— In a large saucepan or deep fryer, bring the frying oil to 300°F (150°C). Dip a flat ladle into the oil to heat it to the same temperature. Use a fork or chopsticks to form a nest of sweet potato strips in the ladle. Pour a little batter over the strips and carefully arrange one shrimp on top. Plunge the ladle into the oil for 5 minutes. Remove the fritter and drain on paper towels or in a strainer. Repeat the process to make 12 fritters. Just before serving, plunge them again into the oil, heated to 350°F (180°C), for 3 minutes, or until golden. Drain on paper towels.

— Serve on a bed of lettuce and accompany with the herbs and the spring roll dipping sauce.

Cà tím xào tía tô

Preparation time: 20 minutes

Cooking time: 20 minutes

TIPS

• You can make a vegetarian version of this dish by omitting the pork and substituting the fish sauce with 1 teaspoon of salt.

•• If you use cherry tomatoes, there is no need to core and seed them.

••• You need at least ¾ inch (1 cm) of oil in the pan in order to fry the tofu well on each side.

— Peel and cut the shallots into rings. Heat 3 tablespoons (40 g) of the sunflower oil in a deep skillet over medium heat and sweat the shallots. Slice the pork belly and brown in the skillet •. Stir in the salt.

Cut the eggplant into about ½-inch (1-cm)-thick rounds, then cut into quarters. Add to the skillet, mix, and cook for 5 minutes over low heat.

Core and seed the tomatoes ••. Cut into thin wedges and add to the skillet. Mix, cover with a lid, and cook for 10 to 15 minutes over low heat.

— Heat the remaining 1½ cups (330 g) sunflower oil in a saucepan to 350°F (180°C) •••. Fry the whole tofu in the oil for about 10 minutes, turning it over regularly, until golden brown. Drain and let it cool, then thinly slice.

Add a little water or broth to the skillet containing the eggplant if it is too dry. Add the fried tofu, minced garlic, and nuoc mam.

Cut the tia to and rau ram leaves into strips, add to the skillet, and mix carefully to avoid crushing the vegetables. Season with pepper and serve very hot.

2 to 3 shallots (50 g)

1½ cups plus 3 tablespoons
(370 g) sunflower oil

3½ ounces (100 g) pork belly

½ teaspoon (3 g) salt

1 large eggplant
(1¼ pounds/600 g)

4 firm tomatoes
(1 pound 2 ounces/500 g)

5 ounces (140 g) firm tofu

2 cloves garlic (6 g), minced

2 teaspoons (10 g) nuoc mam
(fish sauce)

10 tia to (Vietnamese perilla)
leaves

20 rau ram (Vietnamese
cilantro) leaves

Freshly ground black pepper

SERVES
4

phần 1) Bánh Cốm

gạo - ½ Kg nếp vo.

- 2 bát ăn phở n
- 1 tý màu xanh -
- 2 soupe đầy dàu
  nấu thành cốm he
  với giã nhiên -

phần 2) chờ 1 Kg cốm m
ngập nước cho mềm

phần 3) chờ cốm nếp
+ cốm ngàm +
1 Kg 200 đường + 1 b
nước soupe nấu tan
1 nằm dừa + 1 go
fécule de pomme de te
6 thìa soupe bột năng
hoa biển quấy như bát

The time passed quickly and we found ourselves unable to manage. So I
        started knocking on the doors of the village to ask women
        for help. I gathered about twenty cooks. It was no longer
        about cooking a pot of rice porridge every day, but hun-
        dreds of pots to feed thousands of soldiers. Reluctantly I
        was becoming an important figure in the village.

I would pray every day at the Thai Ha church in Hanoi. I was seeking peace
        for my country, but also my own inner peace. I felt God's
        call and considered becoming a nun.

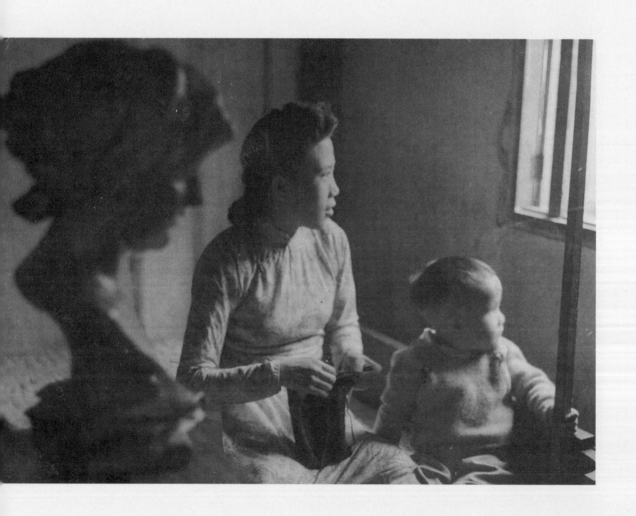

There was a very elegantly dressed man at the church who kept trying to catch my attention and who smiled at me all the time. He made me laugh because he would wear the same white suit every day. That immaculate white suited his tan skin so well. One day, he plucked up the courage and approached to greet me.

At the time, the dông—the local currency—was being devalued. I went to the bank, and Ông was waiting for me there. He had been riding his bike around the neighborhood for hours, anticipating my arrival. At the entrance to the bank, just as we were about to enter, someone opened the door and said "Good morning sir, good morning madam." He liked that, and so did I.

A _yes_ was reverberating deep inside my heart, yet how could I be sure he was the one? I was still being courted by suitors. "If you're shy, say no and I'll take it to mean yes!" he said. I finally answered him bluntly, "Yes is yes, and no is no." But I did say yes to Ông, your grandfather, and I married him. He was poor, but his heart made him rich. Love needs no proof or justification. If he can make you laugh, then it's a sure thing.

Sổ tay Nội trợ

Chả cá Hànội

<u>Vật liệu</u>

Cá lotte hay congre (chọn miếng ít xương)
Bún nhỏ (vermicelle)
Thìa là (fenouil branche)- Lạc rang
Hành lá (vài nhánh) - Rau salade - Thơm mùi - dưa chuột -
Giá sống
Hành tây (oignon) - 2 củ échalotte
Mắm tôm - Poudre nghệ (safran) - Hạt tiêu - nước mắm - Bột
ngọt - Một chén nhỏ dầu (huile de table)

<u>Cách làm</u>

... ... thái từng miếng dầy chừng 3, 4 li bề
... ... đĩa trộn với I thìa café nhỏ nấm
... ... Bột ngọt (hành, échalotte, vài
... ... ộn đều để ngấm chừng 2,3 giờ.
... ... được)
... ... ăng , xong rồi ngâm dấm.

... . Thơm mùi.
... ... a với chanh ớt.
... ... thì càng ngon không thì
... ... u cá vào brochette rồi
... ... ể lửa to cho chóng vàng.
... ... salade. Thái thìa là
... ... lên trên đĩa cá - Trong
... ... lên trên cá. Ăn với bún,
... ... tôm hoặc nước mắm pha vừa

Minh Châu

Ông would take me out in the evening for a chả cá, a Hanoi specialty made with fish and dill. The French brought us this unusual herb. Dill adds a great deal of flavor to this dish.

2¼ pounds (1 kg) monkfish

6 to 7 cloves garlic (20 g)

2 (1¾-inch/4.5-cm) pieces fresh turmeric (20 g)

1¼-inch (3-cm) piece galangal (1½ ounces/40 g)

½ teaspoon (2 g) ground black pepper

1½ tablespoons (20 g) Hanoi-style mam tom (shrimp paste)

7 ounces (200 g) dried rice vermicelli noodles (the same as used for Bo Bun on page 84)

Salt

10 to 12 scallions (160 g)

4 small bunches dill (60 g)

1 large cucumber

½ cup (80 g) unsalted roasted peanuts

3 tablespoons (40 g) sunflower oil

1⅓ cups (300 g) Spring Roll Dipping Sauce (page 211)

Preparation time: 40 minutes

Cooking time: 15 to 20 minutes

Resting time: 1 hour

TIPS

• The mam tom has a very pungent smell, but it is not noticeable in this dish.

•• You can add mam tom, chile, and lime to the dipping sauce if you like.

— Cut the monkfish into ½-inch (1.5-cm) pieces and set aside in the refrigerator.

Peel the garlic, turmeric, and galangal. Use a mortar and pestle to grind to a paste, along with the pepper and mam tom • . Strain through a fine-mesh strainer, keeping only the liquid. Pour this marinade over the fish, mix well, and refrigerate for 1 hour.

— In the meantime, prepare the noodles. Fill a large saucepan with 4¼ cups (1 liter) cold water. Add the noodles and a pinch of salt, and bring to a boil over medium heat. Cook for 5 to 10 minutes. Turn off the heat, cover, and let stand for 5 minutes. Drain, rinse in cold water, and set aside. Mince the scallions and dill. Thinly slice the cucumber. Use a mortar and pestle to crush the peanuts.

Immediately before serving, take the monkfish out of the refrigerator. Heat a large skillet, add the sunflower oil, and sweat the scallions. Add the dill, followed by the pieces of marinated fish. Cook for 5 to 7 minutes, until the fish is cooked through.

Serve hot in a bowl drizzled with spring roll dipping sauce and accompanied with the noodles, cucumber, and peanuts •• .

Chả cá

1¾ pounds (800 g) medium whelks

Salt

7 ounces (200 g) rice vermicelli noodles

1 shallot (15 g)

¾-inch (2-cm) piece ginger (1 ounce/30 g)

1½ tablespoons (20 g) sunflower oil

4 teaspoons (20 g) nuoc mam (fish sauce)

Freshly ground black pepper

2½ tablespoons (60 g) tamarind pulp

12 rau ram (Vietnamese cilantro) leaves

Broth

1 shallot (20 g)

½-inch (1-cm) piece ginger (20 g)

3 tablespoons (40 g) sunflower oil

3⅓ cups (800 ml) Chicken Broth (page 213)

3⅓ cups (800 ml) whelk cooking water

1 cup (6 ounces/160 g) cherry tomatoes, assorted colors

Bún ốc

NORTHERN VIETNAM

**Preparation time:
30 minutes
Cooking time: 1 hour
Resting time: 2 hours**

TIP
• Popular in Europe, whelk are sea snails that may be found fresh along the Atlantic coast in the northeastern United States or in some places along the Pacific coast. Substitute geoduck clam or conch meat if you cannot locate them.

SERVES 4

— Soak the whelks • in a bowl with water to cover and 2 tablespoons salt for 2 hours. Rinse, drain, and set aside.

Fill a large saucepan with 4¼ cups (1 liter) cold water. Add the noodles and a pinch of salt, and bring to a boil over medium heat. Cook for 5 to 10 minutes. Turn off the heat, cover, and let stand for 5 minutes. Drain, rinse in cold water, and set aside.

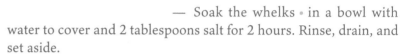

— Put the whelks into a saucepan with 4¼ cups (1 liter) cold water and a pinch of salt. Bring to a boil, then cook for 30 minutes. Use a skimmer to remove the whelks from the pan and strain the cooking water for the broth and reserve. Drain the whelks, then remove the operculum (protective disk) and intestines. Peel and thinly slice the shallot. Peel a ¼-inch (5-mm) piece of the ginger, then use a mortar and pestle to crush it. Brown the whelks in a pan with the sunflower oil, shallot, and ginger. Deglaze the pan with the nuoc mam, then season with a grinding of black pepper.

Soak the tamarind in warm water or chicken broth for 10 minutes. Strain the liquid through a fine-mesh strainer.

FOR THE BROTH

— Peel and thinly slice the shallot and sweat with the ginger in a saucepan with the sunflower oil. Add the chicken broth, then the whelk cooking water. Halve the cherry tomatoes and add them to the pan. Cook for 5 minutes, then add the tamarind liquid and stir to dissolve.

ASSEMBLY

— Thinly slice the remaining ½-inch (1-cm) piece of ginger and the rau ram leaves. Divide the noodles among four bowls, then add the whelks, fresh ginger, and three sliced rau ram leaves per bowl. Season with a pinch of pepper. Pour the hot broth over the noodles and serve immediately.

BÁNH DẺO NHÂN ĐẬU XANH TRỨNG MẶN

hạt dừa   50 grs
mè rang   50 grs
đậu xanh(cả vỏ)   200 grs
hột vịt muối   8 cái
mỡ thịt   100 grs
hạt điều   50 grs
mứt bí   50 grs
đường hạt nhỏ   120 grs

Cách 1

Mỡ luộc ... g café đường, 1/2
muỗng muối để trước ...ăng lấy tròng
đỏ, 50cc nước với 1 ... sết bỏ hột vịt
muối vỏ nấu thêm 5 ... sạch vỏ đem hấp
chín xay nhuyễn, để ... độ 3 phút , cho
các thứ— hạt dừa, ...t,(mứt bí, hạt
điều thái hạt lựu)vào, ... vào nặn lại làm
nhân gói hột vịt vào giữa, cân nhân 60 grs cả hột vịt thì bớt 100 grs

Nhân bánh
(8 cái bánh)

đậu xanh   200 grs cả vỏ
đường nhỏ hạt   200 grs

One evening, when your grandfather came home from work, he told me we would be going to Huế to meet his family and to move closer to the government led by President Diem. I listened to what he had to say, and then I took the opportunity to tell him that I was expecting our first child.

CENTRAL VIETNAM

CENTRAL VIETNAM

CENTRAL VIETNAM

CENTRAL VIETNAM

CENTRAL VIETNAM

CENTRAL VIETNAM

+ 14/8/52

Long,

thầy đã gửi cho
con nhiều lá thơ
rồi, mà sa... thấy
đổi mà không thấy
con mà ... cho
thầy ... thấy
gửi cho con biết
anh, lúc thấy ...
... xem một trai
linh công-binh
gặp rồi cao-miên.
... tìm ra

The journey by train took twenty hours. It was the first time I had left home. I was filled with nostalgia as I watched the landscapes of my country passing before my eyes. I was thinking about my life, my past, my childhood with my parents, my happy adolescence. And about the war. I was sad, because I was leaving behind my best friend, Dang, who was now fully committed to the fight. I felt I was abandoning him by going so far away. But what could I do? I later learned that he was one of the dozen Vietnamese soldiers remaining in <u>Hanoi</u> during the sixty-day battle (fought against the French over control of the city). He was sixteen years old and the youngest of the soldiers. It was his victory; he was a hero.

I thought about the mangoes we would eat together in the evening. And sometimes, when I was overcome with nostalgia, I would cook chicken wings with spicy mango sauce.

Chicken Wings

8 free-range chicken wings

8 cloves garlic

$\frac{2}{3}$ cup (60 g) grated ginger

2 tablespoons (30 g) rice vinegar

1 teaspoon (4 g) salt

$\frac{3}{4}$ teaspoon (2 g) freshly ground black pepper

4 eggs

$1\frac{2}{3}$ cups (200 g) pastry flour

Sunflower oil, for frying

Sauce

$\frac{1}{2}$ ripe mango (100 g)

1 shallot (20 g)

1 bird's-eye chile

1 clove garlic (3 g)

$\frac{1}{4}$ teaspoon (1 g) sugar

$\frac{1}{2}$ teaspoon (2 g) salt

4 teaspoons (20 g) lime juice

MAKES 8 WINGS

Cánh gà chiên giòn

Serves 4

Preparation time: 1 hour
Cooking time: 30 minutes
Resting time: 2 to 24 hours

TIP
• You can add lemon zest
to the marinade.

MARINATING THE CHICKEN WINGS

— Wash the wings well and trim off the excess skin, or remove all the skin if desired. Use a meat cleaver to cut the wings into winglets and drumettes and put them into a dish. Peel the garlic. Peel and mince the ginger. Use a mortar and pestle to crush the garlic and ginger, then add them to the dish with the chicken. Add the rice vinegar, salt, and pepper and mix well •. Cover the dish with plastic wrap and marinate in the refrigerator for at least 2 hours (ideally for 24 hours).

FOR THE SAUCE

— In the meantime, make the dipping sauce. Cut the mango into small dice. Peel and mince the shallot. Seed and finely chop the chile. Peel and grate the garlic with a Microplane grater. In a bowl, mix the mango, shallot, chile, and garlic. Season with the sugar, salt, and lime juice.

COOKING THE CHICKEN WINGS

— Beat the eggs in a bowl. Put the flour onto a plate. Dip each wing piece in the beaten eggs, then dredge in the flour. Heat the oil in a saucepan to 250°F (120°C) and deep-fry the wings until they turn light golden, then remove them from the oil and drain on paper towels. Set aside.
— Immediately before serving, heat the frying oil to 340°F (170°C) and deep-fry the wings a second time until golden brown. Serve accompanied with the dipping sauce.

Huế is the ancient capital of Vietnam. It is also the cradle of Vietnamese
    cuisine. A long time ago, cooks used to prepare meals for
    emperors. Later, their dishes traversed the city walls and
    were made by the common people.
The specialties of this region are dishes wrapped in banana leaves and
    steamed.

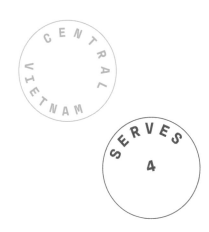
Bánh bèo

**Preparation time:
50 minutes**

**Cooking time: 25 to
30 minutes**

**Resting time: 3 hours
30 minutes**

TIP
• The bowls must be very
hot so that a well forms
in the batter to contain
the filling.

FOR THE BATTER

— Combine both types of flour and the salt in a bowl and add 3 cups (700 ml) water heated to 85°F (30°C). Stir well and let stand at room temperature for 3 hours. Discard the water and add another 3 cups (700 ml) water heated to 85°F (30°C). Let stand for 30 minutes.

FOR THE FILLING

— Peel, wash, and devein the shrimp. Dry well. Peel the garlic and pound to a smooth paste with a mortar and pestle. Put ½ tablespoon of the sunflower oil into a saucepan over high heat and add the shrimp. Season with the salt and sugar, then sear. When almost cooked, add the garlic, reduce the heat to low, and cook for 5 minutes. Remove the shrimp from the heat and let cool. Finely chop the shrimp, return to the pan over low heat, and add the annatto oil. Cook for about 5 minutes, until everything is dry. Set aside.

Thinly slice the scallions. Sweat with the remaining 2½ table-spoons sunflower oil in a saucepan over low heat for 5 minutes, then remove from the heat. Set aside the scallions, along with the cooking oil. Optional: Cook the bacon over medium heat until crispy. Drain on paper towels and cut into small pieces.

COOKING AND ASSEMBLY

— Put four small bowls into the steamer basket of a water-filled steamer and heat until steam appears • . Stir the batter and fill the bowls two-thirds full. Cover the steamer and steam for 3 to 5 minutes, then remove the bowls. Divide up the shrimp and add to the bowls. Add the scallions, the reserved cooking oil, the fried shallots cut into small pieces, and bacon, if using. Serve with the spring roll dipping sauce or a bisque made using the shrimp heads and shells (page 212).

Batter

2¾ cups (440 g) plain rice flour

⅓ cup (60 g) glutinous rice flour

1½ tablespoons (26 g) salt

Filling

1¼ pounds (600 g) raw shrimp

6 to 7 cloves garlic (20 g)

3 tablespoons (40 g)
sunflower oil

1¾ teaspoons (10 g) salt

2 teaspoons (8 g) sugar

1 tablespoon Annatto Oil
(page 212)

3 scallions (40 g)

2 ounces (40 g) bacon (optional)

Accompaniments

⅕ recipe (1 ounce/30 g)
Fried Shallots (page 212)

Spring Roll Dipping Sauce
(page 211) or Shrimp Bisque
(page 212)

Chả tôm

14 ounces (400 g) peeled
raw shrimp (about 1 pound
2 ounces/500 g whole shrimp)

3 cloves garlic (10 g), peeled

1 teaspoon (4 g) nuoc mam
(fish sauce)

Pinch of salt (1 g)

Pinch of ground black pepper (1 g)

4 lengths fresh sugarcane
(³⁄₈ inch/1 cm in diameter)

3 tablespoons (40 g)
sunflower oil

Accompaniments

14 ounces (400 g) rice noodles,
cooked according to package
instructions

10 lettuce leaves

20 sprigs cilantro

1 recipe (⁷⁄₈ cup/200 g) Spring
Roll Dipping Sauce (page 211)

**Preparation time:
40 minutes
Cooking time: 15 minutes**

TIPS

• You can also use a
knife to chop up the
shrimp for the mixture,
but never a food
processor.

•• You can finish cooking
the sugarcane shrimp
by frying in a skillet
or on a grill.

— Wash and drain the shrimp well; they must be very dry. Devein and finely chop the shrimp. Use a mortar and pestle to crush the shrimp to a paste with the peeled garlic, nuoc mam, salt, and pepper • .

— Use your hands to knead the paste, then wrap the paste around each length of sugarcane leaving the ends exposed. Place a steamer basket over a saucepan of water on the heat and wait for the steam to rise. Put the shrimp paste-wrapped sugarcane in the steamer basket and steam for 15 minutes, until the paste looks firm •• .

— Accompany with rice noodles, lettuce leaves, cilantro, and spring roll dipping sauce.

Nem nướng

Preparation time: 1 hour
Cooking time: 1 hour
Resting time: 1 hour

TIP
• You can make smaller
meatballs and cook them
in the oven or on a
grill.

FOR THE MEATBALLS

— Remove and reserve all the fat from the pork and cut the meat into pieces. Use a meat grinder fitted with a fine plate to grind the meat. Refrigerate for 1 hour.

Preheat the oven to 300°F (150°C). Cut the pork fat into ¼-inch (5-mm) cubes (you will need ⅓ cup/80 g) and blanch in a saucepan of water over medium heat. After 5 minutes, turn off the heat and drain. Peel and mince the garlic. In a large bowl, combine the meat with the pork fat, garlic, yeast, potato starch, sugar, pepper, toasted rice powder, and nuoc mam and mix to incorporate the ingredients. Add the egg whites and mix again to make the forcemeat. Shape the forcemeat into 1½-inch (4-cm)-diameter balls and arrange on a baking sheet or oven rack. Place in the center of the oven and bake for 20 minutes. Turn the meatballs over and continue to cook for another 20 minutes. Increase the heat to 400°F (200°C) and brown the meatballs for 5 minutes. Remove from the oven and set aside •.

FOR THE NOODLES

— Fill a large saucepan with 6⅓ cups (1.5 liters) cold water. Add the noodles and a pinch of salt, and bring to a boil over medium heat. Cook for 5 to 10 minutes. Turn off the heat, cover, and let stand for 5 minutes. Drain, rinse in cold water, and set aside.

ASSEMBLY AND SERVING

— Crush the peanuts. Cut the cucumber into thin sticks. Wash and trim the lettuce leaves. Wash and pluck the herbs. Line the inside of a bowl with a lettuce leaf and cover with noodles. Arrange a few nem nướng balls on top. Garnish with the herbs, cucumber sticks, and 1 teaspoon crushed peanuts. Finish with 1 tablespoon spring roll dipping sauce or hoisin sauce.

3 pounds 5 ounces (1.5 kg) fresh ham (pork leg steak)

⅓ cup (80 g) pork fat

1 head garlic (50 g)

2⅓ teaspoons (8 g) active dry yeast

2½ tablespoons (25 g) potato starch

⅓ cup (60 g) sugar

1¾ teaspoons (4 g) ground black pepper

⅓ cup plus 1½ tablespoons (80 g) toasted rice powder

¼ cup (60 g) nuoc mam (fish sauce)

2 egg whites

14 ounces (400 g) rice vermicelli noodles (bun)

Salt

⅓ cup (50 g) salted peanuts

1 cucumber

Lettuce leaves

Herbs: cilantro, tia to (Vietnamese perilla)

Spring Roll Dipping Sauce (page 211) or hoisin sauce (see Bò Bía recipe, page 112)

SERVES 6

Chè trôi nước

**Preparation time:
30 minutes
Cooking time: 25 minutes
Resting time: 1 hour**

TIP
• Depending on the flour you use, you may need more or less water.

1¼ cups (200 g) glutinous rice flour

---

1 teaspoon (5 g) salt, plus more for cooking water

¾-inch (2-cm) piece ginger (30 g)

¾ cup (150 g) cane sugar

---

1 tablespoon (10 g) sesame seeds

— Combine the rice flour with ¾ teaspoon (4 g) of the salt in a bowl, then gradually add ½ cup plus 1½ tablespoons (140 g) water heated to 105°F (40°C) • . Mix and knead the dough; it should be supple, not brittle, and it should not stick to your fingers. Cover with plastic wrap and rest for 1 hour.

— Shape into ¾-inch (2-cm)-diameter dough balls (8 g each). Add them to a saucepan of lightly salted hot water. Cook for about 5 minutes, stirring regularly. The balls are cooked when they float to the surface and have grown in size. Remove them from the pan and refresh by plunging in cold water. Drain and let cool.

— Fill another saucepan with 1 cup (250 g) water and put over medium heat. Peel and cut the ginger into very thin slices. Put into the pan with the sugar and the remaining ¼ teaspoon (1 g) salt. Reduce the heat and cook for 15 minutes. Add the cooled rice balls and let steep in the ginger-flavored syrup for 30 minutes.

Toast the sesame seeds in a small dry skillet for 5 minutes, or until golden. Put six to eight sticky rice balls into a bowl and cover with the candied ginger and syrup. Sprinkle the sesame seeds over the top. Serve warm.

nhan

It is said that the most beautiful girls in the country live in Huế. They are descendants of imperial families, and they have the greatness of kings and the elegance of queens.

I loved hearing all these stories. As your grandfather told them to me, he also explained to me his place in the country. Since he was born in the countryside of central Vietnam, his future was not particularly promising. As the rice paddies were in the north of the country and the economic capital was in the south, he found he was alone on his land. This situation encouraged him to better himself and gradually move up the political ladder.

He knew the countryside, the land where he was born, so well, and he loved it dearly.

SERVES
4

Thịt heo kho

CENTRAL VIETNAM

1¾ pounds (800 g) pork belly (not too fatty)	2 tablespoons plus 2 teaspoons (40 g) nuoc mam (fish sauce)
½ shallot (20 g)	2½ tablespoons (30 g) palm sugar
3 tablespoons (40 g) sunflower oil	3 cups (700 g) chilled coconut water •
¾ teaspoon (4 g) salt	¾ teaspoon (2 g) ground black pepper
3 tablespoons (60 g) Bà's Caramel Syrup (page 208)	4 eggs
2 cups plus 2 tablespoons (500 g) Chicken Broth (page 213)	

Preparation time: 1 hour
Cooking time: 2 hours

TIPS
• Preferably use coconut water without added sugar. If using sweetened coconut water, add less palm sugar.
•• For a marbling effect, crack the egg when halfway cooked and color the water with caramel.

— Cut the pork belly into 2-inch (5-cm) lengths, then trim to rectangular pieces 1¼ inches (3 cm) in width and 1¼ inches (3 cm) thick.

Peel and thinly slice the shallot. Sweat in a saucepan with the sunflower oil over medium heat for 5 minutes. Brown the pork and season with salt. Add the caramel syrup and stir to coat the meat well all over. Cover with the broth. When the scum floats to the surface, after about 15 minutes, remove it using a skimmer or a large spoon.

Add the nuoc mam, palm sugar, and chilled coconut water, then cover with a lid, reduce the heat, and simmer for 1 hour 30 minutes. Remove the lid and simmer for 30 more minutes over medium heat. The sauce will slowly reduce until it thickens. Season with the pepper.

— In the meantime, hard-boil the eggs, then peel them ••. Add to the pan with the caramelized pork 30 minutes before serving.

Thịt heo quay

2¼ pounds (1 kg) pork belly

2 tablespoons (38 g) salt

3 cloves garlic (10 g)

2 tablespoons (25 g) sugar

¾ teaspoon (3 g) five-spice powder

2 tablespoons (30 g) soy sauce plus more for the baking dish

¼ cup (50 g) sunflower oil

1 teaspoon (6 g) rice vinegar

2¼ teaspoons (8 g) active dry yeast

Preparation time: 30 minutes

Cooking time: 1 hour 20 minutes

Resting time: 2 hours 30 minutes

TIP

• The appeal of this dish lies in the crispy skin and the aroma of the spices. It is one of the fillings used to make Bánh Mì (page 152).

— Wash the pork belly. Blanch in a stockpot filled with water and 1½ tablespoons (28 g) of the salt over medium heat. Bring to a boil and cook for 15 minutes. Remove the meat from the pan. Rinse to remove impurities and check that the skin is clean and free of hairs. Dry the meat in a cloth. Peel, degerm, and mince the garlic. Combine the sugar, five-spice powder, and garlic in a bowl and mix well. Add the soy sauce and sunflower oil and mix well. Rub the mixture over the sides of the pork belly, but not the skin. In another bowl, mix the vinegar, the remaining 1½ teaspoons (10 g) salt, and the yeast. Set the pork belly with the skin side facing upward and make sure the surface is very dry. Use a meat tenderizer or bamboo skewer to prick the skin ten times without piercing the fat. Brush the skin with the mixture. Repeat the process several times. Rest the meat in the refrigerator for 2 hours.

— Remove the meat from the refrigerator and let stand at room temperature for 30 minutes. Preheat the oven to 400°F (200°C). Grease an ovenproof dish with oil, then put the meat into the dish, making sure the skin is very dry. Place in the center of the oven and roast for 50 minutes. Increase the heat to 475°F (240°C) and roast for an additional 10 minutes. Finish cooking under the broiler for 3 minutes, watching closely. Remove from the oven and rest • .

— When ready to serve, because the skin is very crispy, you will need to use scissors or a serrated knife to cut the meat. Cut up the pork and serve accompanied with rice and nuoc mam or soy sauce.

Cá chiên

SERVES
4

2 (1¼–1½-pound/600–700-g) wild sea bream, scaled and cleaned

1½ teaspoons (8 g) salt

2 tablespoons (30 g) sunflower oil

2 tablespoons (30 g) nuoc mam (fish sauce)

2 banana leaves

2 bay leaves

Thai basil shoots

Garlic flowers

Sauce

½-inch (1-cm) piece ginger (20 g)

3 cloves garlic (10 g)

2 tablespoons (30 g) nuoc mam (fish sauce)

3½ tablespoons (50 g) lime juice

2 teaspoons (10 g) sugar

1 red chile (optional)

**Preparation time:
10 minutes
Cooking time: 14 minutes**

TIPS
• This recipe can be made using gilthead sea bream, black sea bream, or blackspot sea bream.
•• You can put two slices of lime and two slices of ginger inside the belly of each fish before putting them in the oven.
••• Each fish can be wrapped in a banana leaf and cooked on the grill.

— Preheat the oven to 450°F (230°C). Rub the inside and outside of the fish • with the salt. Mix the sunflower oil with the nuoc mom and brush the fish with the mixture •• . Put each fish on one banana leaf, then bake in the oven for 7 minutes ••• . Turn the fish over and brush again with the sunflower oil–and–nuoc mam mixture if they appear to be too dry. Bake for another 7 minutes.

— In the meantime, make the dipping sauce. Peel and cut the ginger and garlic into small dice. Mix in a bowl with the nuoc mam, lime juice, and sugar. Thinly slice the chile, if using, and add it to the mix.

— Serve the fish with the dipping sauce, a few Thai basil shoots, and garlic flowers.

Mực xào

1¼ pounds (600 g) squid,
cleaned •

4 cloves garlic

⅓ stalk lemongrass (20 g)

4 teaspoons (20 g) nuoc mam
(fish sauce)

5 okra pods (60 g)

1⅓ cups (200 g) cherry
tomatoes, halved

2 garlic scapes (20 g)

12 tia to (Vietnamese perilla)
leaves

3 tablespoons (40 g) sunflower
oil

SERVES 4

**Preparation time:
25 minutes
Cooking time: 5 minutes
Resting time: 30 minutes**

TIP
• You can use cuttlefish
instead of squid.

— Cut the squid into 1¼ by 2½-inch (3 × 6-cm) rectangles, then use a knife to score a diamond pattern. Peel the garlic and mince the lemongrass. Place the squid pieces in a bowl with the nuoc mam, garlic, and lemongrass and marinate in the refrigerator for 30 minutes.

— Cut the okra diagonally into thin slices. Halve the cherry tomatoes and thinly slice the garlic scapes and tia to leaves. Heat the sunflower oil in a skillet over high heat and add the okra. When golden brown, add the marinated squid and sauté for about 5 minutes, until colored. Add the tomatoes, cook for 1 to 2 minutes, then add the garlic scapes. Add the tia to leaves immediately before serving.

Lẩu việt nam

Broth	Accompaniments
4 tomatoes (1 pound 2 ounces/500 g)	1¼ pounds (600 g) rice vermicelli noodles
3 carrots (7 ounces/200 g)	10½ ounces (300 g) beef tenderloin
1¼ stalks lemongrass (80 g)	10½ ounces (300 g) peeled raw shrimp
7 to 8 stalks celery (11 ounces/300 g)	30 mustard greens or iceberg lettuce leaves
¼ pineapple (7 ounces/200 g; cut from the pineapple lengthwise)	1 white onion (3½ ounces/100 g)
1 white onion (3½ ounces/100 g)	1 bunch cilantro
1½-inch (4-cm) piece ginger (50 g)	A few rau ram (Vietnamese cilantro) stems
2 teaspoons (10 g) sunflower oil	**Sauces**
5 teaspoons (30 g) salt	Spring Roll Dipping Sauce (page 211)
3½ tablespoons (40 g) sugar	Pineapple and Anchovy Sauce (page 208)
¼ cup (60 g) distilled white vinegar	
1¼ cups (300 g) coconut water	
2 eggs	

Preparation time: 1 hour
Cooking time: 45 minutes

FOR THE BROTH

— Wash the vegetables. Cut the tomatoes into quarters. Peel and cut the carrots into 2½-inch (6-cm) lengths, then into cubes. Cut the lemongrass and celery diagonally into ¼-inch (8-mm)-thick slices. Peel the pineapple, quarter lengthwise, and cut into strips. Finally, peel and thinly slice the onion, then peel and crush the ginger using a mortar and pestle. In a stockpot, sweat the onions in the sunflower oil, then add the ginger and lemongrass and sauté for 5 minutes. Add all the vegetables except the celery. Season with the salt and sugar, then add 10½ cups (2.5 liters) water and bring to a boil over medium heat. Boil, uncovered, for 30 minutes. Reduce the heat and skim the broth. Add the vinegar, followed by the coconut water and celery. Carefully break the eggs into the broth without mixing. Adjust the seasoning with nuoc mam, if necessary. Continue to cook for 15 minutes, skimming regularly. Keep simmering over low heat.

FOR THE ACCOMPANIMENTS

— Fill a large saucepan with 8½ cups (2 liters) cold water. Add the noodles and a pinch of salt, and bring to a boil over medium heat. Cook for 5 to 10 minutes. Turn off the heat, cover, and let stand for 5 minutes. Drain, rinse in cold water, and set aside.

Slice the beef very thinly. Devein the shrimp (make a shallow slit along the back and remove the black intestine). Wash and trim the mustard greens or lettuce leaves. Peel and very thinly slice the onion.

SERVING

— Put a pot of the broth on an electric hot plate in the center of the table to keep simmering. Arrange the assorted accompaniments and sauces on the table. Use a strainer scoop to cook the shrimp and meat in the broth. Put the noodles and herbs into a large bowl, then add the shrimp and meat and drizzle with sauce. You can also dip the mustard greens or lettuce leaves in the broth. Finally, the broth can be drunk like a soup in small bowls • .

TIP

• Feel free to liven up this firepot with your favorite ingredients, such as chicken, squid, or pork liver. You can also make fresh spring rolls with rice paper wrappers to enjoy with the spring roll and pineapple dipping sauces.

We made the journey to Saigon by car and then train. I remember taking the Mandarin Road from Huế over the Hải Vân Pass, a place where the mist and sun coexist in poetic harmony.

We also spent a few days in Hoi An, a gorgeous little town with yellow houses and a unique fragrance. Then, we finally arrived in the capital, Saigon.

7 ounces (200 g) rice vermicelli noodles

Salt

4 to 6 shallots (100 g)

⅔ cup (150 g) sunflower oil

6 to 7 cloves garlic (20 g)

1 stalk lemongrass (60 g)

1 pound 2 ounces (500 g) beef tenderloin

¾ teaspoon (2 g) ground black pepper

5 teaspoons (24 g) nuoc mam (fish sauce)

1 cucumber

⅓ cup (60 g) roasted peanuts

4 lettuce leaves

Herbs: cilantro, mint, Thai basil leaves

Spring Roll Dipping Sauce (page 211)

SERVES 4

Bò bún

Preparation time: 1 hour
Cooking time: 40 minutes
Resting time: 1 hour
Marinating time: 1 hour

FOR THE NOODLES

— Fill a large saucepan with 4¼ cups (1 liter) cold water. Add the noodles and a pinch of salt, and bring to a boil over medium heat. Cook for 5 to 10 minutes. Turn off the heat, cover, and let stand for 5 minutes. Drain, rinse in cold water, and set aside.

FOR THE FRIED SHALLOTS

— Peel and thinly slice the shallots. Heat the sunflower oil in a saucepan over medium heat, then add the shallots and stir regularly. After 10 minutes, when the oil is simmering, check that the shallots are beginning to lightly color. Strain through a colander and save the oil to cook the meat. Set aside the shallots, which will continue to brown and firm up.

FOR THE MEAT

— Peel and mince the garlic. Thinly slice the lemongrass. Sprinkle the meat with 1¼ teaspoons (8 g) salt. Cut the meat into thin slices, place in a bowl, and marinate with the garlic, lemongrass, pepper, and nuoc mam for 1 hour.

ASSEMBLY AND SERVING

— Cut the cucumber into ¼-inch (5-mm)-thick sticks. Use a mortar and pestle to coarsely crush the peanuts. Pour 2 teaspoons (10 g) of the shallot cooking oil into a hot skillet and cook the meat for about 1 minute, more or less depending on whether you prefer it more raw or more cooked. Shred one lettuce leaf and put into a bowl with the noodles and top with the meat. Add the herbs and cucumber. Top with fried shallots and sprinkle with crushed peanuts. Drizzle with the spring roll dipping sauce • . Repeat for the remaining servings.

TIP
• Spicy food lovers can add sliced chile.
This dish can also be accompanied with spring rolls.
You can also add pickled carrot. Cut a carrot into julienne strips and soak in rice vinegar with salt for 30 minutes. Drain well and add to the bowl.

Gỏi cuốn thịt

SOUTHERN VIETNAM

7 ounces (200 g) dried rice vermicelli noodles

Salt

7 ounces (200 g) beef tenderloin or sirloin

½ cup (100 g) sunflower oil

4 teaspoons (20 g) nuoc mam (fish sauce)

3 cloves garlic (10 g)

2 scallions (30 g)

2 to 3 shallots (50 g)

Fresh cilantro

Garlic chives

Lettuce leaves

1 cucumber

½ stalk lemongrass (25 g)

12 (7-inch/18-cm-diameter) rice and tapioca starch wrappers

Spring Roll Dipping Sauce (page 211)

Preparation time:
20 minutes
Cooking time: 40 minutes
Resting time: 20 minutes

FOR THE NOODLES

— Fill a large saucepan with 4¼ cups (1 liter) cold water. Add the noodles and a pinch of salt, and bring to a boil over medium heat. Cook for 5 to 10 minutes. Turn off the heat, cover, and let stand for 5 minutes. Drain, rinse in cold water, and set aside.

FOR THE MEAT

— Rub the meat with ½ teaspoon (3 g) salt. Heat 2 tablespoons (20 g) of the sunflower oil in a skillet over high heat and sear the meat for 1 minute on each side. Deglaze the pan with 1½ teaspoons (8 g) of the nuoc mam and remove from the heat. Rest the meat for 20 minutes. In the meantime, peel and crush the garlic with a mortar and pestle. When the meat has rested and cooled, cut it into very thin slices, or even strips, or chop into small pieces, then add the garlic and the remaining 2½ teaspoons (12 g) nuoc mam. Mix well and set aside.

FOR THE SCALLIONS AND SHALLOTS

— Thinly slice the scallions. Peel and thinly slice the shallots. Put 3 tablespoons (40 g) of the remaining sunflower oil into a saucepan over medium heat and add the scallions. Cook for 5 minutes, remove from the heat, and set the scallions aside in a bowl. Add another 3 tablespoons (40 g) sunflower oil into the pan and add the shallots. Cook until lightly colored, then drain and set aside. They will continue to cook. Reserve the cooking oil for browning the meat.

FOR THE REST OF THE FILLING

— Wash the herbs and lettuce leaves. Remove the hard ribs from the lettuce and cut the cucumber into three even lengths, and then into thin sticks. Set everything aside. Thinly slice the lemongrass. Heat 2 teaspoons (10 g) of the shallot cooking oil in a skillet and sear the lemongrass for 1 minute. Add the meat and cook for 1 minute, stirring briskly. Remove from the heat.

ASSEMBLY

— Dip each rice paper wrapper into hot water for a few seconds, drain, and lay on a flat plate. Position one lettuce leaf centered at the bottom of the sheet and add about 1 tablespoon (10 to 15 g) rice noodles. Add a few cucumber sticks, followed by the meat, cilantro, lemongrass, and fried shallots. Top with 1 tablespoon scallions and fold one side of the rice paper wrapper over everything. Then add one garlic chive leaf and roll up tightly • . Accompany with the spring roll dipping sauce •• .

TIPS
• You can add crushed peanuts to the summer rolls.
•• You can add chile or tia to (Vietnamese perilla) to the dipping sauce.

Gỏi đu đủ với tôm

SERVES
4

1 large green papaya
(14 ounces/400 g)

2 cloves garlic (6 g)

1½ tablespoons (20 g) sunflower
oil

8½ ounces (240 g) peeled
shrimp tails (small or large)

3 tablespoons (40 g) nuoc mam
(fish sauce)

3½ tablespoons (40 g) sugar

5 tablespoons (80 g) lime juice

20 Thai basil leaves

1½ ounces (40 g) Fried Shallots
(page 212)

Sliced red chile

**Preparation time:
25 minutes
Cooking time: 2 minutes**

— Remove the seeds from the papaya
and grate the flesh. Peel and crush the garlic with a mortar and pestle.
Brown the garlic in a skillet with the sunflower oil over medium heat.
Increase the heat and sear the shrimp, seasoning with the nuoc mam
and sugar.

Mix the papaya with the lime juice in a bowl. Add the shrimp mixture, Thai basil, fried shallots, and chile and serve.

CÔNG-TY
BÍCH-CHI
kính tặng

...ỰC LÀM BÁNH
...vã Bột nếp
...ơn từ các trường
...chánh)

mẫu
thêu

Saigon in 1955 was an amazing place. I felt like I had traveled through time. The South is so different from the North. The city of Saigon was enormous, and it had a special energy. I was fascinated by the Notre-Dame Cathedral Basilica of Saigon, by the post office—built by Gustave Eiffel—and by the opera house, which was directly inspired by the architecture of the Opéra Garnier in Paris.

Nevertheless, it was a time of great misery in Vietnam, during which the French were gradually abandoning the country. I remember having so little money that we generously salted what little meat we were able to buy so we could eat as little as possible, and we ate more rice.

I also cooked a lot of nước canh. This is the name given to a meat or fish broth accompanied with vegetables.

Canh chua cá

SERVES
4

1 shallot (20 g)

1½ tablespoons (20 g)
sunflower oil

5½ cups (1.3 liters) Chicken
Broth (page 213)

2½ tablespoons (60 g) tamarind
pulp

⅔ cup (60 g) prepared de bac
ha (taro stem)

4 to 5 okra pods (60 g)

⅔ cup (100 g) thinly sliced
pineapple

5 to 6 cherry tomatoes (80 g)

3½ tablespoons (40 g) sugar

2 tablespoons plus 2 teaspoons
(40 g) nuoc mam (fish sauce)

9 ounces (260 g) wild salmon
steak

2 cloves garlic (6 g)

⅔ cup (20 g) rice paddy herb
leaves, for garnish

Dill sprigs, for garnish

**Preparation time:
30 minutes
Cooking time: 30 minutes**

TIPS
• You can make this dish
using conger eel, cod,
sea bass, or another type
of fish.
•• If you don't have
rice paddy herb, you can
use lemon basil or fresh
cilantro leaves.

— Peel and thinly slice the shallot. Fry in a saucepan with the sunflower oil. Add the chicken broth. Put the tamarind into a bowl of water and knead it. Strain the liquid through a fine-mesh strainer and add to the broth. Peel the fruits and vegetables. Slice the taro stems into 2-inch (5-cm)-thick rounds and the okra into ½-inch (1-cm)-thick rounds. Add the fruits and vegetables to the broth, season with the sugar and nuoc mam, and simmer for 15 to 20 minutes.

— Clean the fish and cut into 4-inch (10-cm) lengths •. Crush the garlic. Add to the broth along with the crushed garlic and continue to cook for 5 minutes. Transfer to a soup tureen and add the rice paddy herb leaves •• and dill immediately before serving.

SOUTHERN VIETNAM

Canh rau cải

SERVES 4

3¾ cups (900 ml) Chicken Broth
(page 213)

3 cups (180 g) mustard greens

½-inch (1-cm) piece ginger
(18 g)

4 teaspoons (18 g) nuoc mam
(fish sauce)

**Preparation time:
15 minutes
Cooking time: 20 minutes**

TIPS
• If you are making
the broth yourself, the
boiled chicken can be cut
into pieces and used to
make another dish. Enjoy
the greens Saigon style,
dipped in nuoc mam, or
dip them in a mixture
of salt, pepper, and a
drizzle of lemon juice
like they do in Hanoi.

•• The flavor of this
dish, which is typically
light and invigorating,
depends on the mustard
greens you choose. The
younger they are, the
less intense their
flavor.

— In a medium saucepan, bring the chicken broth to a boil over medium heat. Reduce the heat • .

— Wash the mustard greens, separating the leaves from the stems if too thick. Slice the leaves into 4-inch (10-cm) lengths and the thicker stems into ½-inch (1-cm)-thick rounds. Peel the ginger, slice into ¾-inch (2-cm)-thick rounds, then crush using a mortar and pestle. First add the mustard stems to the broth, because they take longer to cook. Add the leaves after 5 minutes. Add the ginger and nuoc mam and continue to cook for 15 minutes. Adjust the seasoning and serve in a bowl • •. This dish can also be accompanied with rice.

Bắp cải xào cà chua

SERVES 4

**Preparation time:
15 minutes
Cooking time: 20 minutes**

½ head green cabbage
(10½ ounces/300 g)

5 tomatoes (1 pound
2 ounces/600 g)

1 to 2 shallots (30 g)

3 cloves garlic (10 g)

2 tablespoons (30 g)
sunflower oil

2 tablespoons (30 g) nuoc mam
(fish sauce)

Fresh cilantro leaves

Freshly ground black pepper

— Remove the outer leaves from the cabbage. Rinse, halve, and remove the core. Thinly slice the cabbage. Wash the tomatoes, remove the stems, and cut into quarters. Peel and thinly slice the shallots. Peel and mince the garlic.

— Heat the sunflower oil in a skillet over medium heat. Sweat the shallots until colored. Add the cabbage, followed by the tomatoes, and deglaze the skillet with the nuoc mam. Add the garlic and cook for 20 minutes, until the cabbage is translucent. Season with a few fresh cilantro leaves and a turn or two of the pepper mill, then serve.

2 cups (350 g) white rice

½ cup (20 g) dried shrimp

1¼ teaspoons (8 g) salt

4¼ ounces (120 g) unpeeled fresh shrimp

2 shallots (40 g)

1½ ounces (40 g) lap cheong (Chinese sausage)

3 tablespoons (40 g) sunflower oil

3 tablespoons plus 1 teaspoon (50 g) soy sauce

½ teaspoon (2 g) five-spice powder

⅔ cup (100 g) fresh shelled peas

3 cloves garlic (10 g)

1½ tablespoons (20 g) butter

SOUTHERN VIETNAM

SERVES 4

Cơm chiên

Preparation time: 1 hour
Cooking time: 30 minutes

TIPS
• To calculate the correct amount of water for the rice as done in Vietnam, pour the rice into a rice cooker, level it out, and place your index finger so that it is touching the surface of the rice. Add enough water so that it comes up to your first knuckle.

•• You can use cubes of roast pork or chicken instead of the shrimp.

••• You can also add scrambled eggs to this dish.

— Wash the rice three times in luke-warm water. Put into a saucepan and add 1½ cups (380 g) water •. Cover and cook over medium heat for 15 minutes. When all the water is absorbed by the rice, reduce the heat to the lowest setting. Using chopsticks, very gently fluff the rice without breaking the grains. Cover and cook for another 20 minutes, then turn off the heat. Fluff the rice again, cover, and let cool.

— Wash the dried shrimp and put into a saucepan with 1 cup (250 g) water •• . Add the salt, then bring to a simmer and cook over low heat for 15 minutes. Remove from the heat and drain the shrimp. Let cool, then chop or crush with a mortar and pestle. Set aside.
  Peel and devein the fresh shrimp. Cut them into ½-inch (1-cm) pieces. Peel and thinly slice the shallots. Cut the lap cheong into large pieces. Heat the sunflower oil in a deep skillet over low heat. Sweat the shallots, then add the sausages and fresh shrimp. Sauté for 5 minutes, then add the dried shrimp. Add the rice to the skillet and mix gently, seasoning with the soy sauce and five-spice powder. Add the peas. Peel and crush the garlic. When everything is heated through, finish with the garlic and butter ••• . Mix again before serving.

SERVES
4

5 tomatoes (1 pound
2 ounces/600 g)

2 to 3 shallots (1½ ounces/40 g)

Sunflower oil

½ cup (100 ml) Chicken Broth
(page 213) or water (optional)

1 teaspoon (10 g) sugar

2 tablespoons (30 g) nuoc mam
(fish sauce)

14 ounces (400 g) firm tofu

10 cloves garlic (30 g)

Freshly ground black pepper

2 small scallions (10 g)

Fresh cilantro

Đậu hũ sốt cà chua

SOUTHERN VIETNAM

Preparation time: 15 minutes
Cooking time: 30 minutes

TIP
• Start by preparing the sauce, and fry the tofu while it is cooking so that both are hot at the same time.

FOR THE TOMATO SAUCE

— Blanch the tomatoes, then peel and seed them. Peel and thinly slice the shallots. Heat 1½ tablespoons (20 g) sunflower oil in a saucepan and sweat the shallots. Add the tomatoes and cook for 5 minutes to soften. Add the chicken broth or water, if necessary, if the tomatoes do not release enough juice. Season with the sugar and nuoc mam, then let reduce over low heat •.

FOR THE TOFU

— Cut the tofu into four ¾-inch (2-cm)-thick rectangles. Heat ½ inch (1 cm) sunflower oil in a saucepan to 350°F (180°C). Fry the tofu for about 15 minutes, turning over several times, until golden on all sides. Use a skimmer to remove the tofu from the oil, drain, and set aside.

ASSEMBLY

— Peel and mince the garlic. After cooking the sauce for 20 minutes, when the tomatoes are reduced to the consistency of a puree, add the garlic, followed by the tofu. Season with a sprinkling of pepper and heat for 5 minutes. Thinly slice the scallions and pluck the cilantro. Sprinkle over the dish immediately before serving.

In the evening, I would sometimes buy a dessert to take home from the small food stall on the corner of my street, where a young woman with a big smile would prepare chè chuối, a dessert made with banana, for me.

Chè chuối

SERVES 6

SOUTHERN VIETNAM

2 tablespoons (20 g) roasted peanuts

1 tablespoon (10 g) white sesame seeds

½ teaspoon plus ⅔ teaspoon (7 g) salt

1⅔ cups (400 ml) coconut milk

2 tablespoons plus 2 teaspoons (25 g) tapioca pearls

1 cup (200 g) sugar

2 teaspoons (8 g) vanilla sugar

4 bananas (1½ pounds/700 g)

Preparation time: 15 minutes
Cooking time: 20 minutes

TIP
• Use ripe bananas, because they have more flavor.

— Use a mortar and pestle to coarsely crush the peanuts. In a dry skillet, toast the sesame seeds with ½ teaspoon (3 g) of the salt over low heat for 5 minutes.

Combine the coconut milk with ½ cup (100 ml) water in a saucepan. Stir, then add 1½ tablespoons (20 g) of the sugar and ¼ teaspoon (2 g) salt. Stir again and set aside.

Heat 4¼ cups (1 liter) water in a saucepan to 175°F (80°C). Add the tapioca pearls while stirring gently to prevent them from sticking together. Cook over medium heat for 10 to 20 minutes, until the pearls become translucent. Add the remaining sugar, remaining salt, and vanilla sugar and cook over low heat. Peel the bananas and cut on the diagonal into ¾ to 1¼-inch (2 to 3-cm)-thick slices • . Add to the tapioca and cook for 10 minutes. Then add the coconut milk, stir, and cook for another 2 minutes.

— Spoon a ladle of the tapioca-and-banana dessert into six individual bowls and sprinkle each serving with a little of the toasted sesame seeds and crushed peanuts. Serve warm.

Cà phê sữa đá

1 cup (250 ml) black coffee

⅓ cup (80 ml) condensed milk or evaporated milk, or more to taste

5 to 6 ice cubes

Makes about 1½ cups (350 ml)
Preparation time: 10 minutes
Cooking time: 10 minutes

In Vietnam, we use a special individual coffee filter. The ground coffee is placed inside the container and held over a glass by a metal disk. Hot water is poured over the coffee, which drips into the glass. This beverage is to be drunk cold, either sweetened or unsweetened.

— After making black coffee as desired, pour it into a glass with a capacity of 1½ cups (350 ml). Add the condensed or evaporated milk and stir. Adjust to taste, then add the ice cubes. Enjoy.

Tướng Weede viếng thăm
Ha. C. V. VL.   8 - 6 - 62

12297

12299

Ông worked hard. His motto was "Tri, Dung, Thanh" ("Intelligence, Valor, Sincerity"). He had an unwavering faith that the country would be reunified. Events gathered pace with the departure of the French and the arrival of the Americans. Sometimes he would come home discouraged.

We had four children, and I was expecting the fifth. With the diapers, church, and cooking, I was kept busy, despite the help I received from the nanny. To lift his spirits, I made your grandfather his favorite soup, the one his mother would cook for him: bún bò Huế, the traditional soup of the Huế region.

When he was alone in his yard, your grandfather dreamed of a land at peace. He imagined himself living in a large house surrounded by his family and loved ones. What he hoped for the most was to see a free Vietnam.

Bún bò huế

TIPS

• It is important to use Huế-style mam tom when making this dish, but its pungent smell may be unpleasant to certain people. You can put a sealed container of it on the table for everyone to use as they please.

•• This soup is eaten with a lot of chile in Huế. You can spice it up by adding chile powder after serving.

Preparation time: 1 hour
Cooking time: 2 hours

---

2 (14-ounce/400-g) packages rice vermicelli noodles for bún bò Huế

3¼ pounds (1.5 kg) pig's feet (cut into four pieces by the butcher)

---

3 to 5 shallots (75 g), plus 1 or 2 (30 g) shallots for assembly and finishing

---

4 stalks lemongrass (250 g)

½ cup (120 g) sunflower oil

2¼ pounds (1 kg) rib steak

2¼ pounds (1 kg) ham hock

---

5 tablespoons (90 g) salt

---

2 tablespoons (20 g) annatto (achiote) seeds

1½ tablespoons (20 g) Huế-style mam tom (shrimp paste)

---

5 cloves garlic (15 g)

---

2 tablespoons plus 1 teaspoon (40 g) nuoc mam (fish sauce)

1¼ teaspoons (3 g) ground black pepper

---

2 white onions (7 ounces/200 g)

Herbs: cilantro, rau ram (Vietnamese cilantro)

---

3 limes, cut into wedges (optional)

FOR THE NOODLES

— Soak the noodles in lukewarm water for 45 minutes, or until soft, then drain. Fill a stockpot with 8¼ quarts (8 liters) water and add 3 tablespoons (55 g) of the salt and the noodles. Bring to a boil, then turn off the heat, cover with a lid, and let stand for 15 minutes. Drain, rinse in cold water, and set aside.

FOR THE MEAT

— Wash the pig's feet. Fill a stockpot with 5 quarts plus 1 cup (5 liters) water, place over high heat, and add the pig's feet to blanch them. When the water comes to a boil, boil for 15 minutes, or until scum floats to the surface. Remove the meat and rinse with clean water. Discard the blanching water.

FOR THE BROTH

— Peel and thinly slice the 3 to 5 shallots. Thinly slice the lemongrass. Heat 1½ tablespoons (20 g) of the sunflower oil in the pot over medium heat. Add 2⅔ cups (180 g) of the lemongrass and the shallots, then sweat. Add 4¼ quarts (4 liters) water and the rib steak. Season with 2 tablespoons plus 1 teaspoon (40 g) salt, cover with a lid, and simmer for 50 minutes. Skim the broth, then remove the meat and set aside. Reserve the beef broth.

In the meantime, put 4 quarts plus 1 cup (4 liters) water into another stockpot. Add the pig's feet, ham hock, and 5 teaspoons (30 g) salt. Simmer over medium heat for 1 hour, or until the skin is supple. Skim, if necessary, then remove the meat. Set aside both the meat and pork broth.

When the meat has cooled, cut the steak and ham hock into ⅛-inch (3-mm)-thick slices. Heat 6 tablespoons (80 g) of the remaining sunflower oil in a saucepan over low heat and add the annatto seeds. Cook for 5 to 10 minutes, then strain the red oil and set aside. Add the seeds to the beef broth, followed by 8½ cups (2 liters) pork broth. Heat the broth over medium heat, then add the mam tom, pig's feet, and ¼ cup (50 g) annatto oil • . Simmer for 40 minutes, or until the pig's feet are very soft. Remove the pig's feet.

ASSEMBLY AND FINISHING

— Peel and thinly slice the remaining 1 to 2 shallots. Peel and crush the garlic. Heat the remaining 1½ tablespoons (20 g) sunflower oil in a deep skillet and sauté the shallots, garlic, and remaining lemongrass for 5 minutes. Add the ham hock and beef slices, 2 tablespoons (30 g) annatto oil, and the nuoc mam. Gently stir. Season with pepper and set aside.

Thinly slice the onions. Pluck and mince the rau ram and cilantro leaves. Put the noodles into a bowl and add some beef, ham hock, and pig's feet. Season with a sprinkling of pepper and add the hot broth, wetting the contents of the bowl. Add the herbs and onion and serve with a lime wedge on the side, if using • • .

SERVES 4

Vegetables

3½ ounces (100 g) shiitake mushrooms

1 small white onion (2¼ ounces/60 g)

1 leek (3½ ounces/100 g)

½-inch (1-cm) piece ginger (20 g)

1 large carrot (3 ounces/80 g)

1½ stalks celery (2¼ ounces/60 g)

3 tablespoons (40 g) sunflower oil, plus more as needed

2 cloves garlic (6 g)

5 teaspoons (24 g) soy sauce

2 tablespoons (30 g) nuoc mam (fish sauce)

1 teaspoon (14 g) sesame oil

1 tablespoon (20 g) oyster sauce

Fresh cilantro

Crispy noodles

3½ ounces (100 g) Chinese egg noodles

4¼ cups (1 liter) sunflower oil

1 tablespoon (8 g) cornstarch

Mì giòn xào rau

Preparation time:
30 minutes
Cooking time: 40 minutes

TIPS
• If you like spicy food,
you can add sriracha hot
sauce to the dish.

•• You can make this
a vegetarian dish by
substituting fish sauce
with 2 teaspoons of salt.
You can also supplement
this dish with chicken
or shrimp if you like.

FOR THE VEGETABLES
— Soak the mushrooms in lukewarm water for 30 minutes. Drain and thinly slice. Peel all the vegetables. Thinly slice the onions and leeks. Cut the ginger into 1¼-inch (4-cm)-long matchsticks and the carrot into thin strips. Cut the celery on the diagonal into slices. Heat the sunflower oil in a saucepan and brown the onions. Remove and set aside. In the same pan, repeat the process with the leeks, followed by the ginger, mushrooms, and, finally, the celery. Add a little more oil between each batch, if necessary.

Peel and crush the garlic. Mix all the vegetables in the pan and add the garlic, soy sauce, nuoc mam, sesame oil, and oyster sauce. Set aside • .

FOR THE CRISPY NOODLES
— In a saucepan, soak the noodles in lukewarm water for 30 minutes, or until soft. Drain and set aside. Heat the sunflower oil for deep-frying in a saucepan. Mix the fresh noodles with the cornstarch and shape into a nest on a skimmer. Immerse the skimmer in the very hot oil for 2 minutes, or until crispy, then drain the noodles on paper towels. Repeat the process to make four crispy noodle nests.

ASSEMBLY AND FINISHING
— Place a crispy noodle nest on each plate, then arrange the vegetables on top. Garnish with cilantro •• .

Bò bía

**Preparation time:
30 minutes**

Cooking time: 45 minutes

TIPS

• If you are unable to find fresh brick pastry, you can use rice and tapioca starch wrappers. Soak in hot water to soften before rolling.

•• In August in Vietnam, the sweeter and tastier cu dau (jicama or Mexican potato) is preferred for this dish.

••• For lovers of spicy food, sriracha hot sauce can be added.

FOR THE FILLING

— Wash and peel the carrots and chayotes ••. Cut into 2-inch (5-cm) pieces and then into 1⁄16-inch (2-mm)-thick julienne strips. Heat 2 cups (500 ml) water in a saucepan over low heat and add the sausages. Cook for 10 minutes, then drain. Cut into 2-inch (5-cm) lengths and then into 1⁄16-inch (2-mm)-thick julienne strips.

Wash and drain the dried shrimp. Put into a pan with 2 cups (500 ml) water and 1 teaspoon (8 g) of the salt and cook over medium heat for 15 minutes. Drain and let stand, then coarsely chop.

Peel and thinly slice the shallot and garlic. Heat the sunflower oil in a deep skillet and sweat the shallot. Add the sausage strips and cook over low heat for 5 minutes. Add the carrot and chayote strips and chopped dried shrimp. Add the remaining 1 tablespoon (16 g) salt, the hoisin sauce, and garlic and cook for 15 minutes. Crush the peanuts.

FOR THE OMELET

— Beat the eggs and cook in a skillet to make a thin omelet. Let cool, then cut it into long thin strips.

FOR THE ROLLS

— Lay one brick pastry sheet on a plate and cover the bottom two thirds with a tablespoon (10 g) of the filling and 1 to 1½ teaspoons (5 g) of the omelet. Add a little crushed peanut and a cilantro leaf. Starting from the bottom edge, partly roll up the sheet very tightly. Fold each side over and finish rolling. Set aside.

FOR THE DIPPING SAUCE

— Heat the hoisin sauce in a small saucepan over low heat. Add 3½ tablespoons (50 g) water, the garlic, coconut water, and sugar •••. Cook for 5 minutes. Dip the bò bía rolls in the sauce.

SERVES 6

5 carrots (10½ ounces/300 g)

4 chayotes (1¾ pounds/800 g) or jicama

4¼ ounces (120 g) lap cheong (Chinese sausages)

3¾ cups (150 g) dried shrimp

4 teaspoons (24 g) salt

1 shallot (12 g)

8 cloves garlic (25 g)

1½ tablespoons (20 g) sunflower oil

4 teaspoons (20 g) hoisin sauce

⅓ cup (50 g) salted roasted peanuts

2 eggs

50 fresh brick pastry sheets (6¼-inch/16-cm squares) •

1½ cups (25 g) cilantro leaves

Dipping Sauce

⅓ cup (100 g) hoisin sauce

3 cloves garlic (8 g)

3½ tablespoons (50 g) coconut water

2 teaspoons (8 g) sugar

SERVES
4

7 ounces (200 g) rice vermicelli noodles

Salt

1 medium-large red onion (5 ounces/140 g)

3 tablespoons (45 g) sunflower oil

2 tablespoons plus 2 teaspoons (40 g) soy sauce

1 teaspoon (4 g) sesame oil

1½ tablespoons (10 g) grated young ginger

4 teaspoons (20 g) rice vinegar

3 ounces (80 g) raw shrimp

1 teaspoon (5 g) nuoc mam (fish sauce)

4 sprigs cilantro

½ cucumber

4 spring roll rice and tapioca wrappers (7–8½ inches/18–22 cm in diameter)

4 sucrine (Little Gem) lettuce leaves

8 mint leaves

4 spring onions

Spring Roll Dipping Sauce (page 211)

Gỏi cuốn

**Preparation time:
30 minutes
Cooking time: 10 minutes**

TIP
*• You can add smoked
paprika to the onions
for a smokier flavor.*

FOR THE NOODLES

— Fill a large saucepan with 4¼ cups (1 liter) cold water. Add the noodles and a pinch of salt, and bring to a boil over medium heat. Cook for 5 to 10 minutes. Turn off the heat, cover, and let stand for 5 minutes. Drain, rinse in cold water, and set aside.

FOR THE RED ONIONS

— Peel and thinly slice the onion. Sauté in a skillet with 2 tablespoons of the sunflower oil until caramelized. Deglaze the skillet with the soy sauce, then add the sesame oil, grated ginger, and rice vinegar • .

FOR THE SHRIMP

— Heat the remaining tablespoon of sunflower oil in a skillet. Shell the shrimp and cook for 4 minutes, until they turn pink. Deglaze with the nuoc mam. Set aside. Halve the shrimp lengthwise, deveining them.

ASSEMBLY

— Mince the cilantro. Cut the cucumber in half, scoop out the seeds, and cut into matchsticks. Boil water and pour it into a large bowl. Soak a rice paper wrapper in the hot water, then lay on a flat surface, such as a plate. Position a lettuce leaf centered at the bottom of the sheet and cover with ⅓ to ½ ounce (10 to 15 g) rice noodles. Then add caramelized onions, some minced cilantro, two mint leaves, one spring onion, and a little cucumber, followed by two shrimp, arranging them so they will be visible through the wrapper. Roll very tightly from the start, folding down the sides in the process. Repeat the process to make another three rolls. Serve with the spring roll dipping sauce.

Dough

3¼ cups (400 g) pastry flour

4 eggs

¼ teaspoon (2 g) salt

Filling

10½ ounces (300 g) pork belly

3 scallions (40 g)

1-inch (2.5-cm) piece ginger (40 g)

1¼ cups cilantro leaves (20 g)

¾ teaspoon (2 g) ground black pepper

2 tablespoons (30 g) nuoc mam (fish sauce)

Salt

3½ tablespoons (50 g) soy sauce

2 teaspoons (10 g) brown rice vinegar

1 teaspoon (5 g) sesame oil plus 2 teaspoons (10 g) sesame oil for pan-frying (optional)

2 tablespoons (30 g) sunflower oil for pan-frying (optional)

Hoành thánh nhân thịt

**Preparation time:
45 minutes**

**Cooking time:
3 to 4 minutes**

Resting time: 30 minutes

TIPS

• You can use store-bought wonton wrappers instead of making the dough yourself.

•• You can replace the pork belly in the filling by grinding 10½ ounces (300 g) skinless free-range chicken.

FOR THE DOUGH

— In a large bowl, mix the flour with the eggs and salt. Knead the dough for 10 to 15 minutes, until smooth. Cover with plastic wrap and let stand for 30 minutes at room temperature •.

FOR THE FILLING

— Grind the meat. Thinly slice the scallions, peel and mince the ginger, and mince the cilantro. Mix well with the meat and season with the pepper and nuoc mam ••.

COOKING AND ASSEMBLY

— Pass the dough through a pasta machine. Use a cookie cutter to cut out 3½-inch (9-cm)-diameter disks. Put a generous tablespoon of the filling in the middle of each disk, then fold to make the dumplings. Moisten the edges so that they stick.

Pour 4¼ cups (1 liter) water into a saucepan and add a pinch of salt. Cook the dumplings for 3 to 4 minutes, until translucent, then drain. Serve immediately with a dipping sauce made with the soy sauce, brown rice vinegar, and the 1 teaspoon (5 g) sesame oil. Alternatively, pan-fry them with a mixture of the sesame oil and sunflower oil for a few minutes in a covered skillet.

và vật liệu. Nói tóm lại, chúng ta có thể giúp con cháu chúng
ta tiến bộ rất nhiều nếu ta ý thức được tầm quan trọn của

N.'', mà đưa và rước các c

đó là chưa nói đến những

các cháu có được những dụng

máy rọi hình, máy ghi âm,

ương pháp mới, tập hát tiếng

cần thiết cho việc tổ chức

ác cháu, vì các cháulàtương

ha mẹ nào yêu con mình,muốn

dồi dào tình cảm đối với

n đề giáo dục con em mình

i và Nhi đồng đang góp phần

các người phụ trách, đểkết

HÔNG TIN LIÊN LẠC

dược tiền ủng hộ của các
nh thật cám ơn :

	200 F
	113 + 200 F
- Bà Hoàng Xuân Hẫn	300 F
- Bà Soje Đào thị Yến	50 F
- Ba Đỗ Thị Minh	50 F
- Bà La Postocle Mẫo	50 F

In order to raise the profile of Ông's convictions, together we created
a newspaper that we called *Tieng Dan*, "the Voice of the
People." I was the publisher and editor-in-chief of this
newspaper for three years. It allowed Ông to publicize
his project and his political intentions.

I would go to the <u>market</u> every morning. After attending church, it was
    my daily meeting place. I love markets for the smell of
    spices, the fresh herbs and local produce, and for the
    people you meet there.
Tia to (Vietnamese perilla), rau ram (Vietnamese cilantro), cilantro, mint,
    Thai basil—these are the treasures of Vietnamese cuisine.

In the same way that French women chat with each other as they string
    their green beans, Vietnamese women meet in their yards
    to sort and pluck herbs.

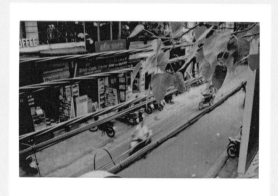

You may be wondering why your mother loves cà, pickled eggplant, so much. Well, I used to eat a lot of it when I was pregnant with her. Sometimes it annoyed your grandfather so much that he would do anything to try to stop me from eating it.

SERVES 4

Pickled eggplant

1 small green eggplant
(7 ounces/200 g)

2½ teaspoons (15 g) salt

Spring Roll Dipping Sauce
(page 211)

5 cloves garlic, peeled

Pickled carrots and turnips

1 Roscoff or white onion

2 turnips or 3 carrots
(7 ounces/200 g)

½ cup (120 g) rice vinegar

1 tablespoon (20 g) salt

¼ cup (50 g) sugar

Pickled mustard greens

2¼ pounds (1 kg) mustard
greens (not too young for
a better crunch)

3 small white onions
(9 ounces/250 g)

⅓ cup plus 1 tablespoon (80 g)
sugar

3 tablespoons plus 1 teaspoon
(60 g) salt

Đồ chua

**Preparation time:
5 minutes
Cooking time: 3 hours
Resting time: 3 days**

**Makes about 1¼ cups
(200 g) pickles
Preparation time:
5 minutes
Resting time: At least
1 hour**

**For 2¼ pounds (1 kg)
leaves
Preparation time:
10 minutes
Resting time: 4 to 5 days
plus 2 to 6 hours**

TIP
• These pickles can be
kept in their pickling
liquid for one week in
the refrigerator.

FOR THE PICKLED EGGPLANT

— Cut the eggplant lengthwise into eight pieces. Place on a baking sheet and dry out in a convection oven at 175°F (80°C) for 3 hours. Rub the eggplant with the salt, then rinse in water and drain. Marinate the eggplant pieces in the spring roll dipping sauce with the garlic in a sealed jar for 3 days •.

FOR THE PICKLED CARROTS AND TURNIPS

— Peel and thinly slice the vegetables. Soak the vegetables in a mixture of the vinegar, salt, and sugar for at least 1 hour and up to 1 week. Drain well before serving •.

FOR THE PICKLED MUSTARD GREENS
Note: Make 4 to 5 days before eating.

— Dry out the mustard greens depending on the season: 30 minutes under the sun in summer, 1 hour over a radiator in winter. They must be well dried. Wash two or three times in plenty of water, then cut into 2½ to 3¼-inch (6 to 8-cm)-long pieces.

Peel and thinly slice the onions. Pour 10½ cups (2 liters) water into a saucepan over medium heat and dissolve the sugar and salt. Turn off the heat and set aside until the temperature of the water drops to 100°F (40°C). Make alternating layers of mustard greens and onions in a 2-quart (2-liter)-capacity jar until the ingredients are used up. Pour the water at 100°F (40°C) into the jar to completely cover the vegetables. If necessary, use a small bowl or cup to weigh down the vegetables so that they are constantly covered. Seal the lid tightly and rest for 4 to 5 days. These pickled mustard greens can be dipped in nuoc mam (fish sauce) and enjoyed, and they are also the basic ingredient of Canh Rau Cải (Mustard Green Soup; page 94) •.

QUYẾT TÂM THEO LÃNH-TỤ   Thành Tín   MỘT DẠ VỚI NON SÔN

KÍNH CẨN CHAO MỪNG TỔNG-THỐNG VIỆT-NAM CỘNG-HÒA

By 1962, the situation had become more complicated. The Americans were willing to do anything to win the war. Ông's policies and those of President Diem were struggling to make sense. The communists dressed like civilians, so it was difficult to identify them in the strategic hamlets the government was building. Gradually, the North Vietnamese, the Viet Minh, gained ground as the Americans tried to take control. We were in danger; the pressure was growing.

But I had Ông and our nine children, and we were together. That was the most important thing.

My family was the greatest of my treasures.

After attending church, we would buy these little pork or vegetable pies. That is how I rewarded the children. They loved it, especially Quy.

MAKES
20
PIES

Pastry dough

2 (8-ounce/230-g) rolls puff pastry

1 whole egg

2 egg yolks

Vegetable filling

1 to 2 shallots (25 g)

¼-inch (5-mm) piece ginger (10 g)

1 large red bell pepper (6 ounces/170 g)

⅔ chayote (4½ ounces/130 g)

2 cloves garlic (6 g)

1½ tablespoons (20 g) sunflower oil

2½ tablespoons (40 g) hoisin sauce

2 teaspoons (10 g) soy sauce

¼ teaspoon (.5 g) ground black pepper

2½ tablespoons (2.5 g) cilantro leaves

Meat filling

3 ounces (80 g) chicken livers

1 shallot (20 g)

2 cloves garlic (6 g)

5 ounces (150 g) ground pork loin (or veal, but it is drier)

¾ teaspoon (2 g) ground black pepper

2 teaspoons (10 g) nuoc mam (fish sauce)

Bánh patê sô

Preparations: 30 minutes
Cooking time: 30 minutes
for meat and 25 minutes
for vegetables
Resting time: 30 minutes

Take the puff pastry out of the refrigerator 1 hour before use.

FOR THE VEGETABLE FILLING
— Peel and mince the shallots and ginger. Wash the bell pepper and chayote and finely dice. Peel and crush the garlic. Heat the sunflower oil in a skillet over medium heat and sweat the shallot. Add the chayote and cook for 5 minutes, stirring constantly, then add the bell pepper, followed by the ginger. Add the garlic, hoisin sauce, soy sauce, and black pepper. Thinly slice the cilantro leaves and add to the skillet after 10 minutes. Stir. When the vegetables are cooked but still remain firm, remove from the heat and let cool.

FOR THE MEAT FILLING
— Cut the livers into small cubes. Peel and mince the shallot. Peel and crush the garlic with a mortar and pestle. In a bowl, gently mix the ground pork with the livers, shallot, pepper, nuoc mam, and crushed garlic. Set aside.

ASSEMBLY AND BAKING
— Preheat the oven to 350°F (180°C). Roll out the puff pastry. Use a cookie cutter to cut 40 disks 2¾ inches (7 cm) in diameter for meat pies, or 3¼ inches (8 cm) in diameter for vegetable pies. Beat the egg. Using a spoon, shape about 1 tablespoon (15 g) meat filling or 1 tablespoon (20 g) vegetable filling into a ball and place in the center of one of the pastry disks. Brush around the filling with beaten whole egg and cover with a second pastry disk. Gently press with your fingers to join the two disks, then use the tines of a fork to seal the rim, making an attractive pattern. Repeat the process to make 20 pies. Arrange on a baking sheet lined with parchment paper. Bake the meat pies for 30 minutes and the vegetable pies for 25 minutes, then remove from the oven and let stand for 5 minutes. Brush each pie with beaten egg yolk and return to the oven for 10 to 15 minutes. Take the pies out of the oven, let cool a little, and serve.

Bánh xèo

Makes 10 crepes
**Preparation time:
30 minutes
Cooking time: 35 minutes
Resting time: 3 hours**

FOR THE MUNG BEANS

— Rinse the beans in cold water and put into a bowl. Fill the bowl with water over the top of the beans and add ½ teaspoon (3 g) of the salt. Let stand for 3 hours, then drain. Put the beans into a saucepan and cover again with water over the top of the beans. Cook over medium heat for 30 minutes, or until the water has been absorbed or evaporated. Remove from the heat and drain. Use a mortar and pestle to grind the beans to a paste. Adjust the seasoning with the remaining ½ teaspoon (3 g) salt, if necessary. Set aside.

FOR THE BATTER

— Put the rice flour into a bowl, then gradually whisk in the beer. Add ⅓ cup plus 1½ tablespoons (100 ml) cold water, the turmeric, salt, coconut milk, and scallions.

ASSEMBLY

— Heat 2 tablespoons (30 g) of the sunflower oil in a skillet over high heat. Put 1 ounce (30 g) of meat into the hot pan and fry for 1 minute. Add ¾ ounce (20 g) shrimp, 1 tablespoon (10 g) sliced white onion, 3 tablespoons (20 g) bean sprouts, and about ¼ cup (80 g) crepe batter. Carefully push the filling toward one side of the pan. Cook for 2 minutes, then add the mung bean paste and bean sprouts. When everything is well cooked, fold the crepe in half. Reduce the heat and cook for another 2 minutes, or until crispy. Remove from the pan and drain. Repeat the process to make 10 crepes.

— Serve each hot crepe with two lettuce leaves, three tia to leaves, three mint leaves, and cilantro, with the spring roll dipping sauce. Add a chile if desired • .

Mung beans

½ cup (100 g) mung beans

1 teaspoon (5 g) salt

Batter

1¼ cups (200 g) rice flour

1 cup (250 ml) lager beer

1 teaspoon (2 g) ground turmeric

1 teaspoon (5 g) salt

¼ cup (50 g) coconut milk

4 scallions, green part only, thinly sliced

Filling

1⅓ cups (300 g) sunflower oil

10½ ounces (300 g) pork belly

7 ounces (200 g) shrimp

1 white onion (3½ ounces/100 g), thinly sliced

2 cups (200 g) bean sprouts

20 Batavia or butter lettuce leaves

30 tia to (Vietnamese perilla) leaves

30 mint leaves

20 sprigs cilantro

Spring Roll Dipping Sauce (page 211)

Chile pepper (optional)

SERVES
4

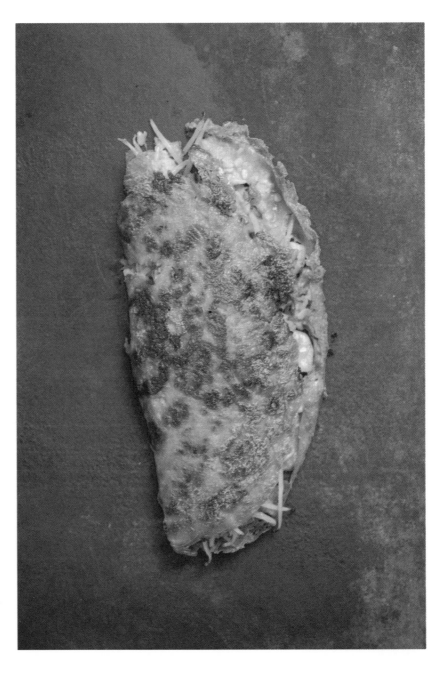

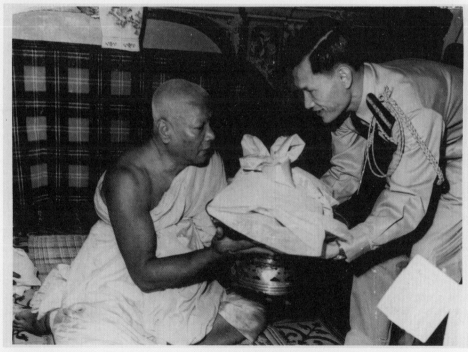

In Saigon, Ông held the position of director of Psychological Warfare under President Diem. They often met in the evening to decide on military strategies. I no longer wanted to hear about politics. During that time, I would stay at home and look after the children. Little Lộc was still a newborn, and the older ones would help the younger ones. Although the situation was deteriorating very quickly, I didn't want to leave. However, on September 9, 1962, we all flew to the United States. I thought leaving on 9/9 with 9 children would bring me luck. Ông was to become the military attaché to the Vietnamese Embassy in Washington, D.C., to oversee military operations in Vietnam from the United States. It was a turning point.

From the plane, I took one last look at the country of my childhood that had made me so happy, and it broke my heart to leave. The Catholics and the Buddhists in Vietnam had been in a permanent state of conflict. Thich Quang Duc, a Buddhist monk, was the first person to self-immolate as a protest against the Diem regime. It was dreadful. Economic rivalry had turned into a religious war. The American intervention did not foretell a peaceful future. I felt that this power could destroy our country, and it was heart-wrenching. I was thinking about Dang. What was to become of him? Did he still have the same self-assurance and the same determination? Or had he given up? No, he would never do that. I knew he would do his best, and I prayed for him.

A 13 734 870   *This is to certify that*
REGISTRATION NUMBER

Phuoc Tai NGUYEN

was admitted to the United States as an immigrant

on	05	01	64		WAS
	MONTH	DAY	YEAR		PORT

Z-2	Date of Birth	10	06	60	M
TYPE		MONTH	DAY	YEAR	SEX

and has been duly registered according to law.
Commissioner of Immigration and Naturalization
UNITED STATES DEPARTMENT OF JUSTICE

We moved into a house on Washington's famous Connecticut Avenue. This new environment was a world away from the simpler way of life in Vietnam. I didn't belong there. I was thinking of my people who were at war. Was I being true to myself? I didn't have time to question myself; we no longer had any choice. We now had to assimilate.

I would reminisce about my father carrying me on his shoulders to eat phở in the morning, then I would look at myself in the mirror wearing fitted Vietnamese dresses—the famous *ao dai*, the traditional Vietnamese dress with its little triangle through which you can make out a few inches of flesh. Behind my makeup, I knew what kind of woman I was and where I came from.

Some time later, Ông wanted to move. He no longer wanted to live in the embassy district for a very simple reason: He preferred to pay the rent on a house himself. So we moved from Connecticut Avenue to a working-class district, to one of Washington's Black neighborhoods.

Finding noodles for phở and the essential Vietnamese ingredients became an odyssey. I remember that when we arrived, we had our food confiscated at customs. We had nothing left, but we were together. I thought about our good fortune, and I wanted us to be worthy of it. On weekends, Ông and I would leave the children with the nanny, and we would take the bus from Washington to New York. What a shock it was to see such a high-rise city. It hurt my neck. "Watch where you're going," Ông would keep repeating. At only four feet seven inches (140 centimeters), I was nothing more than a little ant. An ant alone in a foreign land.

I bought dozens of packages of noodles for phở in Chinatown, and I bought myself a bánh bao for the bus trip home. It was my own little treat.

Steamed bun dough

1⅓ cups (170 g) all-purpose flour

3¼ tablespoons (40 g) sugar

1¾ teaspoons (5.5 g) active dry yeast

1½ teaspoons (7 g) sunflower oil

⅓ cup (75 g) water

Filling

¾-inch (2-cm) piece ginger (30 g)

10½ ounces (300 g) beef (cut for roasting)

2 tablespoons (30 g) soy sauce

3½ tablespoons (50 g) sunflower oil

Tamarind Sauce (page 211)

Nuoc mam (fish sauce)

Red chile, minced (optional)

4 radishes

Fresh cilantro

Pickles

1 Roscoff or white onion

¼ cucumber (80 g)

1 small carrot

1½ cups (360 g) distilled white vinegar

3 tablespoons plus 1 teaspoon (60 g) salt

¾ cup (150 g) sugar

MAKES 4 BAO BURGERS

This recipe is made using traditional ingredients but with a modern twist.

Bao burger

**Preparation time:
45 minutes
Cooking time: 25 minutes
Resting time: 2 hours
(for the dough)
plus 30 minutes**

TIP
*• If you're in a rush,
you may be able to buy
the dough balls from a
bakery.*

FOR THE STEAMED BUNS
— Make a well in the flour and add the sugar, yeast, and oil. Gradually add the water while kneading into a dough. Cover with a damp cloth and rest for 2 hours. Shape the dough into pieces the size of a Ping-Pong ball, then steam for 20 minutes in a steamer or a steam oven • .

FOR THE MEAT
— Peel and cut the ginger into pieces. Marinate the meat in a mixture of the soy sauce, 1½ tablespoons (20 g) of the sunflower oil, and the ginger for 30 minutes. Heat the remaining 2 tablespoons (30 g) sunflower oil in a skillet and sear the meat on all sides over high heat so that it is browned on the outside but still very rare or even raw on the inside. Refrigerate for 30 minutes. Cut into long thin strips.

FOR THE PICKLES
— Peel and thinly slice the onion. Cut eight thin slices of cucumber, and use a vegetable peeler to shave thin slices of carrot. Soak everything in a mixture of the white vinegar, salt, and sugar for 30 minutes. Drain well before serving.

ASSEMBLY AND FINISHING
— Cut each steamed bun crosswise to open and spread one of the cut sides with tamarind sauce. Fill with one-fourth (75 g) of the beef strips and season with a little nuoc mam, and chile, if using. Add the pickles. Thinly slice the radishes into rounds and add. Garnish with fresh cilantro and serve.

The President

requests the pleasure of the company of

Mr. and Mrs. Chau

at a reception to be held at

The White House

Wednesday afternoon, May 8, 1963

from 4:00 to 5:00 o'clock

Ông had a very full schedule. So it was up to me to learn English quickly. He was so busy that he asked me to attend receptions in his place. It meant that I was the mother of nine children during the day and a woman of the world in the evening, forced to socialize in a language I couldn't speak. It seemed like such a long time since I was under the mango tree talking with my friend Dang, at sunset, telling each other our dreams. On the other side of the world, I would put on my stiletto heels and drill myself with the only English sentence I knew: "Nice to meet you. My name is Thang." This life was obviously not the one I had imagined, but I had a big, united family.

One evening, as the situation in Vietnam worsened, we invited members of the American government over for dinner. I was petrified. What would we be able to say to one another, since I didn't speak a word of English? Then a small voice whispered in my ear: "Impress them with the food of your country; Hanoi is your friend."
I chose a very simple menu. My mother always told me that simplicity is the greatest of virtues. Spring roll appetizers, duck breast with bamboo shoots, and water spinach accompanied with white rice as an entrée, followed by fruit and sesame candy for dessert.

½ ounce (15 g) dried rice
vermicelli noodles

¼ cup (5 g) dried wood ear
mushrooms

1 onion (3½ ounces/100 g)

5½ ounces (150 g) ground pork
shoulder

½ cup (50 g) shredded carrots

1 egg

2 teaspoons (10 g) nuoc mam
(fish sauce)

⅓ teaspoon (2 g) fine salt

¾ teaspoon (2 g) freshly ground
black pepper

About 15 rice paper wrappers
(6¼ inches/16 cm in diameter)

4¼ cups (1 liter) sunflower oil

A few lettuce leaves

Cilantro

Mint

Spring Roll Dipping Sauce
(page 211)

MAKES ABOUT 15 ROLLS

Chả giò thịt heo

**Preparation time:
30 minutes
Cooking time: 20 minutes**

TIP
• To strengthen the
wrapper when rolling,
add a strip of rice paper
(about one-fifth of a
wrapper) to the bottom.

FOR THE FILLING

— Soak the vermicelli and mushrooms separately in warm water for 30 minutes. Coarsely cut the vermicelli and finely dice the mushrooms. Peel and thinly slice the onions. In a bowl, mix the ground meat with the shredded carrots, onion, noodles, chopped mushrooms, and beaten egg. Season with the nuoc mam, salt, and pepper.

FOR THE SPRING ROLLS

— Boil water and pour into a large bowl. Soak a clean cloth in the water, wring it out, and lay over a table or large tray. Soak a rice paper wrapper in the hot water and lay out over the cloth •.

Make a ¾-ounce (20-g) ball of filling, about 2 teaspoons, and place it centered at the bottom of the wrapper. Partly roll up the wrapper tightly around the filling and flatten the sides to remove any air. Fold the sides over and finish rolling. Repeat the process to make fifteen rolls.

COOKING AND FINISHING

— Heat the sunflower oil to 210°F (100°C) in a saucepan. Lower five rolls at a time into the pan, then gradually increase the heat to 300°F (150°C) without touching or moving them until they turn light golden. Then remove and drain off the excess oil in a colander or on paper towels.

Before serving, deep-fry again at 350°F (180°C) in the same oil for 2 to 5 minutes, depending on the color, then drain. Serve with a lettuce leaf, fresh cilantro, mint, and spring roll dipping sauce.

Vịt xào măng

Preparation time: 1 hour
Cooking time: 1 hour
Resting time: 1 hour

TIP
• If you like duck breast lightly cooked, simply sear in a saucepan.

FOR THE MARINADE
— In a bowl, combine the soy sauce with the five-spice powder, sugar, and crushed garlic. Mix well. Put the duck breasts onto a plate and coat with the marinade. Rest for 1 hour.

FOR THE MEAT
— Trim the duck breasts and remove a little of the fat. Set aside the fat and scraps for the accompaniments. Season the meat with the salt. In a skillet over low heat, color the breasts on their skin side for 10 minutes, being careful not to darken them, then turn over. Continue to cook for 7 minutes over very low heat •. Rest the meat for 20 minutes. Set aside the melted fat to cook the vegetables.

Preheat the oven to 400°F (200°C). Cook the whole duck breasts in the oven for 20 to 30 minutes, depending on the desired level of doneness.

FOR THE VEGETABLE ACCOMPANIMENTS
— Soak the mushrooms in lukewarm water for 30 minutes. Cut off and discard the stems and thinly slice the caps. Set aside 1¼ cups (80 g) for pan-frying and the remainder for the simmered vegetables.

Thinly slice the bamboo shoots lengthwise. If using bamboo shoots preserved in a salty liquid, blanch in boiling water for 5 minutes. If using fresh, blanch for 15 minutes three times, changing the water each time to remove the bitterness. Set aside 1⅓ cups (200 g) for pan-frying and the remainder for the simmered vegetables.

Peel and thinly slice the onions and garlic. In a saucepan, sweat the onion and garlic in the melted duck fat, then add the halved carcasses, duck scraps, and mushrooms. Increase the heat, sauté the contents of the pan until colored, and add the bamboo shoots, soy sauce, cinnamon, and chicken broth. Cut the duck into 3¼-inch (8-mm)-thick slices and add to the pan. Cover with a lid and simmer for 1 hour.

In a skillet, pan-fry the reserved mushrooms and bamboo shoots to an attractive golden color, then add to the duck. Season with pepper before serving.

Marinade

3½ tablespoons (50 g) soy sauce

½ teaspoon (2 g) five-spice powder

1 teaspoon (4 g) sugar

2 cloves garlic (6 g), crushed

Meat

2 free-range duck breasts

⅓ teaspoon (2 g) salt

Vegetable accompaniments

7 ounces (200 g) dried shiitake mushrooms

1¼ pounds (600 g) bamboo shoots (about 1 fresh shoot or two 8-ounce/225-g cans)

1 small onion (2 ounces/60 g)

6 cloves garlic (20 g)

2 duck carcasses (from your butcher)

¼ cup (60 g) soy sauce

1 cinnamon stick (3 g)

5½ cups (1.3 liters) Chicken Broth (page 213)

Freshly ground black pepper

SERVES 4

Rau muống

**Preparation time:
15 minutes
Cooking time: 10 minutes**

1¼ pounds (600 g) water spinach

4 to 6 shallots (120 g)

3 tablespoons (40 g) sunflower oil

Pinch of salt (1 g)

1 tablespoon (16 g) nuoc mam (fish sauce)

6 cloves garlic (20 g)

— Trim the water spinach stems, leaving about 5 inches (12 cm) with the tip, then cut into four pieces lengthwise. Leave the tip as is, with the leaves.

— Peel and mince the shallots. Sweat in a skillet over medium heat with the sunflower oil and salt. Add the water spinach and increase the heat. Add the nuoc mam and sauté over high heat for 5 minutes.

— In the meantime, peel and crush the garlic with a mortar and pestle. When the water spinach is almost cooked, add the garlic and cook for another 2 to 3 minutes.

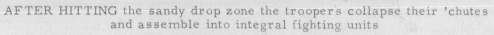

AFTER HITTING the sandy drop zone the troopers collapse their 'chutes
and assemble into integral fighting units

The meal served to the members of the government was a real feast, in their own words. They were won over. However, that day—when I felt I had given the best of myself to honor my family, my husband, and my roots—was also the day when things in my life started to go downhill. President Diem and his brother were assassinated shortly afterward. It was a plot, a coup d'état backed by the Americans and orchestrated by local Vietnamese in this land that had given us refuge. At the same time, Ông lost his brother. Your grandfather never recovered from this loss.

That day had therefore marked the beginning of a long and slow descent into agony. Not only had we lost a president, a friend whom we loved, and a brother, we no longer felt welcome here, in this country that had betrayed us. I felt overwhelmed, with nine children to feed and Ông unemployed. He was wounded and desperate.

Antiwar demonstrations abounded in the streets of Washington, D.C. I secretly dreamed of joining them to express my anger and rage. This atrocious war had to end. I didn't want to return to Vietnam again; I was ashamed.

Misfortune is a long, dark tunnel. Ông resigned and we were going to have to start over, yet again. I prayed for hours and hours and days on end to find a solution. If you trust in God, he hears and answers your prayers. Secours Catholique, the relief services of the Catholic Church in France, offered to help bring us to France; we arrived there in 1964 as political refugees.

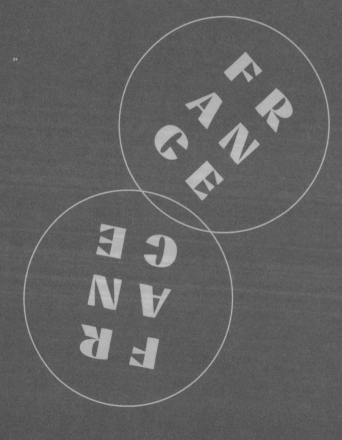

tiền Tây)

H làm ngọ

)[người Tâ

mh)

- nếu muốn làm nhưn lột : mức bí, lột đi
mức hột sen, hột dừa rang, mè, dừa, c
mức ủ năng ... (tùy ý)

I was leaving a big city for a village! We lived in a small market town near Blois, called Mer. It was pretty, despite the gray skies. After learning English, we now had to learn French. Fortunately, Ông could speak a little. But I didn't want to make the same mistakes as I had in the United States. So as soon as we arrived, I wanted us to become fully integrated. It was essential for me.

Later, Ông told me a horrible truth. We were able to rent a house cheaply because a dead man had been found there before we arrived. This is a terrifying thing for a Vietnamese woman because we believe in ghosts!

But I didn't lose my smile, and I was so happy to again find the French baguettes I had known in Saigon. I felt like I was regaining a part of my land, and I would make bánh mì, which the children absolutely loved.

FRANCE

Bánh mì

Preparation time:
45 minutes

Cooking time:
1 hour 20 minutes

Resting time: 2 hours
30 minutes

---

14 ounces (400 g) cooked
meat, such as Crispy Roast
Pork (page 70), 3½ ounces
(100 g) per sandwich

⅓ cup (2 ounces/60 g) pickled
carrots (page 122)

⅓ cup (2 ounces/60 g) pickled
turnips (page 122)

---

1 clove garlic (3 g)

Fresh cilantro

⅓ extra-long cucumber
(1½ ounces/40 g)

---

4 (10-inch/25-cm) baguettes

Maggi sauce or soy sauce

Freshly ground black pepper

---

1 red chile (4 g), sliced
(optional)

Mayonnaise

---

1 egg yolk

---

2 teaspoons (10 g)
Dijon mustard

⅓ teaspoon (2 g) rice vinegar

Pinch of salt (.5 g)

⅔ cup (130 g) sunflower oil

---

2 cloves garlic (6 g)

PREPARING THE INGREDIENTS

— Let the cooked meat cool and cut into thin slices. Make the vegetable pickles, adding a garlic clove to the marinade. Drain well. Wash and pluck the cilantro. Cut the cucumber into slices ⅛ inch (3 mm) thick and 10 inches (25 cm) long, the length of the bánh mì.

FOR THE MAYONNAISE

— Beat the egg yolk in a bowl, then whisk in the mustard, vinegar, and salt. Add the oil in a continuous stream while whisking the mayonnaise until thick and fluffy. Peel and remove the green core from the garlic cloves. Pound in a mortar and add to the mayonnaise. Set aside in the refrigerator.

ASSEMBLY

— Drain the pickles well. Cut each length of baguette crosswise to open. Spread a thin layer of mayonnaise over both cut sides. Divide the crispy pork slices and pickles among the sandwiches, then add two cucumber slices and fresh cilantro. Season with Maggi sauce or soy sauce, then season with pepper. You can also add a little sliced red chile.

MAKES 4 SANDWICHES

say thịt cho nhỏ lửa ... ...
năm Dương Đã có xét, levure, muối vô, bột
gọt, hàn the, tỏi nướng cho vào tròn đều
để trong tủ lạnh một đêm cho ngấm.
... ... say cho nhiễm

pâte ... nước
sl * nếu muốn ... đường ...
... dương ... ngọ...
... lên cho ... đặc ...
... theo nếm miệ...

feuille lau
5-6 gousses d'ail.

It wasn't an easy time for us, but we were never bored. Ông and I promised to do everything we could to make sure our children had access to the best schools. Our goal was to provide them with the means to never experience poverty. There was no way they were going to live in the same conditions that Ông and I had lived in.

Our children's names are: Long (dragon), Lân (unicorn), Quy (turtle), Phượng (phoenix), Tùng (fir tree), Loan (a mythological bird), Yến (golden swallow), Tài (talent), and Lộc (prosperity). When we arrived in France, we used their Christian names. They became Michel, Vincent, Joseph, Thérèse (of Lisieux), Jean, Thérèse (of Avila), Bernadette, Alphonse, and Paul. I wanted God to be with them and to bring them good fortune.
Later on, they laughed at these French names and used their Vietnamese names again. Too bad for them!

Meanwhile, Ông found a new profession. He became a door-to-door salesman for luxury vacuum cleaners in the region. He would take the train every morning. It was a difficult change, but, as in wartime, there was no choice. I prepared a small lunch box for him every day. He loved ginger chicken. He would say to me, "How can I get so excited about such a simple dish?"

Cơm
gà gừng

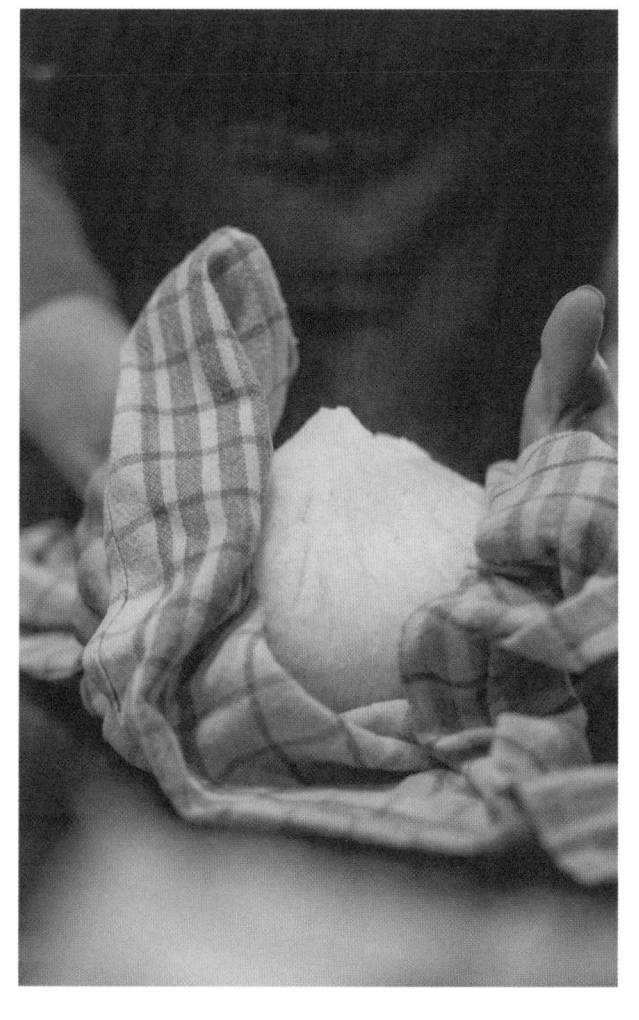

Preparation time:
30 minutes
Cooking time: 30 minutes

---

1 (3¼-pound/1.5-kg) free-range chicken

---

3 tablespoons (40 g) sunflower oil

1-inch (2.5-cm) piece ginger (40 g)

---

1 to 2 shallots (30 g)

---

4 cloves garlic (12 g)

½ teaspoon (3 g) salt

1½ tablespoons (20 g) sugar

---

4 teaspoons (20 g) nuoc mam (fish sauce)

---

1 tablespoon (15 g) Bà's Caramel Syrup (page 208; optional)

½ teaspoon (1 g) ground black pepper

Rice cakes

3¼ cups (600 g) white rice

TIP
• This dish can be accompanied with slices of fresh cucumber.

FOR THE CHICKEN

— Wash and dry the chicken, then cut it into 2½- to 3¼-inch (6- to 8-cm) chunks. Heat 1½ teaspoons (20 g) of the sunflower oil in a saucepan and brown the chicken pieces for about 10 minutes. Remove from the pan and set aside. Reuse the pan for the vegetables.

— Peel and cut the ginger into thin matchsticks. Peel and slice the shallots. Peel and thinly slice the garlic. Heat the remaining 1½ teaspoons (20 g) oil in the pan and sweat the shallots. Add the ginger, and then the chicken, and stir over low heat. Season with the salt, sugar, nuoc mam, garlic, and caramel syrup, if using. Stir, cover with a lid, and cook over low heat for 30 minutes, until the chicken is golden brown and cooked through.

FOR THE RICE CAKES

— Wash the rice three times in luke-warm water. Put into a saucepan and pour in 3 cups (750 g) water. Cook over medium heat for 15 minutes and cover with a lid. When all the water is absorbed by the rice, reduce the heat to the lowest setting. Using chopsticks, very gently fluff the rice, without breaking the grains. Cover and cook for another 20 minutes, then remove from heat. Fluff the rice again, cover, and let cool for 10 minutes.

— Moisten a clean cloth and spread over the work surface. While the rice is still warm, put it in the middle of the cloth, then gather the corners to close. Holding the cloth firmly, knead the rice into a firm ball. Let cool completely wrapped in the cloth. Remove the cloth and use a wet knife to cut into ½-inch (1.5-cm)-thick slices.

— Season the chicken with the pepper and adjust the seasoning as desired. Serve with the rice cakes • .

Thịt bò xào đậu

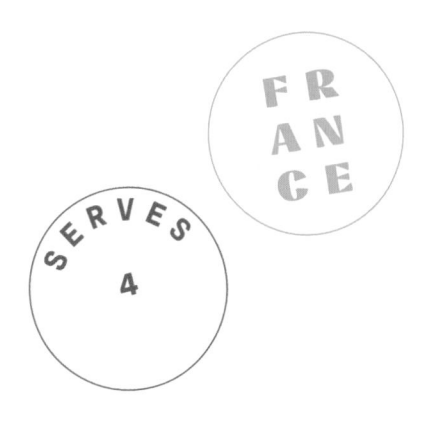

SERVES 4

FRANCE

10½ ounces (300 g) sirloin
or rib steak

⅓ teaspoon (2 g) salt

3 tablespoons (40 g)
sunflower oil

3 cloves garlic (10 g)

1 shallot (20 g)

4 cups (400 g) green beans

2 tablespoons (30 g) nuoc mam
(fish sauce)

¾ teaspoon (2 g) ground
black pepper

**Preparation time:
10 minutes
Cooking time: 15 minutes
Resting time: 10 minutes**

TIP
• You can also make this dish with peas. In that case, it is not necessary to blanch them.

— Pat the meat dry with a sheet of paper towel, removing as much moisture as possible. Sprinkle each side with half of the salt and rub it in well. Heat 1½ tablespoons (20 g) of the sunflower oil in a skillet over high heat. When hot, sear the meat on each side, then remove it. Let the meat cool, then thinly slice it.

— Peel and mince the garlic. Peel and mince the shallot. String the green beans and blanch in a saucepan of boiling water •. Then sauté in a skillet with the remaining 1½ tablespoons (20 g) sunflower oil. Add the sliced meat, garlic, shallot, and nuoc mam. If you like your meat very rare, cook for 4 seconds, otherwise cook for 1 to 2 minutes.

Season with the pepper and serve.

Then we moved from Mer to Orléans. We lived in the small nearby town of Olivet, in the house that we still own. It was a joy to be back in the city. The children were growing up, and we had very little to offer them, but I gave them all my love.

Ông accepted a position as a supervisor at the Sainte-Croix High School. The former lieutenant-colonel ruled with an iron rod! One day, he covered for an absent teacher, which gave him the opportunity to teach. He would immerse himself in books on history, geography, and civic education in the evening on his way home from work. He was preparing for his master's degree in history so that he could become a teacher. However, there wasn't enough money coming in, so I offered to work.

I would open La Hanoïenne, one of the first *tables d'hôtes*, private restaurants, in France, in our family home in 1971. So there was no need to borrow money from a bank, and I could continue to take care of the children.

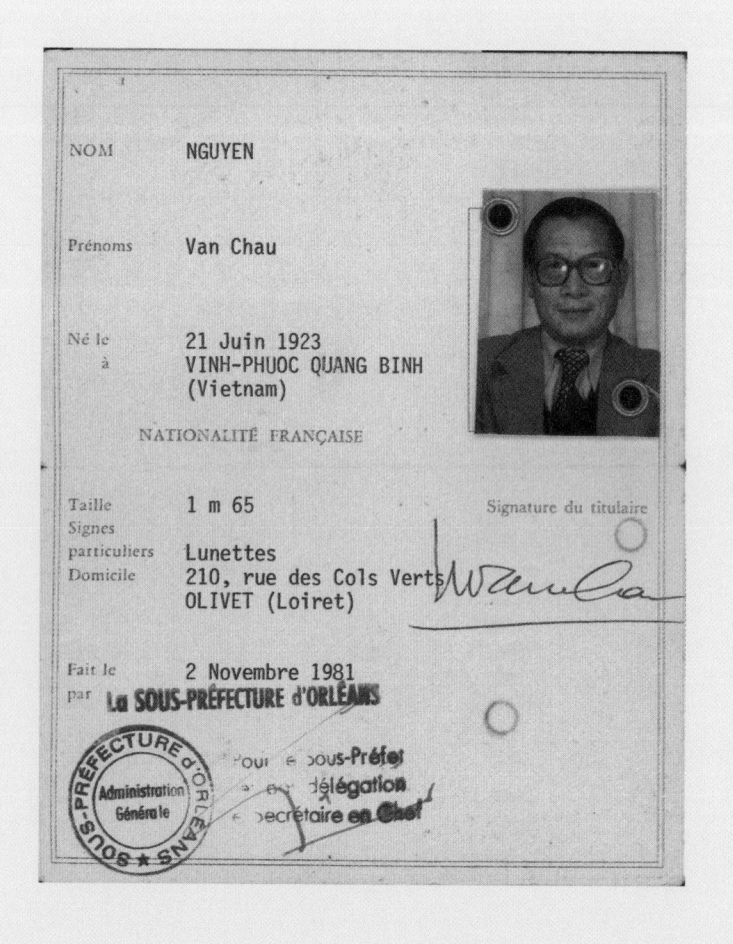

I would take the train to Paris every week. It was my moment of free-
                dom. I love taking the train, but I love Paris even more.
                What a marvelous city. I would stroll across the bridges,
                and I would watch the Bateaux Mouches cruise past the
                Conciergerie. I would walk along the Quai d'Orsay, and
                I would sometimes sit on a bench, look up at the sky, and
                daydream. Were these clouds the same as the ones over
                Hanoi? Had they crossed continents to get here? I had the
                impression that the sun was loyal to me. It was the only
                thing that still linked me directly to my country. Then
                I would tell myself that Dang was looking at the same sun.
                Sometimes.

Then I would go to visit my friend Mrs. Bac Thing, who helped me to
                broaden my knowledge and prepare dishes that I wasn't
                familiar with at the time.
"It's simple you know; just watch me and you'll learn. There's no need for
                measures; you just have to feel the dishes, to love them,"
                she would say. Cooking with love. I looked at the palms
                of my hands; I thought about my father's rice paddies and
                my mother's gentleness, and that gave me the courage to
                cook. Mrs. Bac Thing taught me to love, with all my heart.

When I returned home, there was uproar. The children were bickering;
                the twins were grumbling about their older brothers; the
                little ones felt abandoned by the older ones, who were
                tyrannizing everybody. In short, we had a little war on
                our hands. Whenever Ông intervened, I preferred not to
                get involved. So, with a heavy heart, I would busy myself
                in the kitchen. I had a business to get off the ground.

13

30

14

30

fouk maxi

cccc

FRANCE

Thịt rim tôm

Preparation time:
20 minutes
Cooking time: 30 minutes

— Peel and thinly slice the shallots. Sweat in a saucepan with the sunflower oil over medium heat.

Thinly slice the meat. Add to the pan and sauté until golden. Stir in 2 tablespoons (30 g) of the nuoc mam and cook for 5 minutes, then add the caramel syrup and mix well. Add the broth, cover with a lid, and cook for 15 minutes. Add the shrimp and cook for another 5 minutes. Season with the pepper, sugar, and the remaining 1 tablespoon (15 g) nuoc mam to bring out the flavor. Slice the scallions and sprinkle over everything.

3 to 5 shallots (80 g)

1½ tablespoons (20 g) sunflower oil

9 ounces (250 g) ground pork shoulder, well marbled

3 tablespoons (45 g) nuoc mam (fish sauce)

3 tablespoons plus 1 teaspoon (50 g) Bà's Caramel Syrup (page 208)

⅓ cup plus 1½ tablespoons (100 g) Chicken Broth (page 213)

9 ounces (250 g) raw shrimp tails (wild if possible), peeled and deveined

¾ teaspoon (2 g) ground black pepper

1¾ teaspoons (7 g) sugar

4 scallions, green part only

"La Hanoïenne" à Olivet

La dizaine de restaurants « Chinois » recensés dans l'agglomération Orléanaise ne se sont implantés qu'après 1975.

C'est à cette date que la péninsule indochinoise a connu de profonds bouleversements politico-militaires provoquant le départ de nombreux habitants venus se réfugier dans les pays occidentaux.

Deux restaurants font exception à cette règle : Le Lotus d'Or, l'ancêtre des restaurants « chinois » d'Orléans, ouvert en 1966 et la Hanoïenne en activité depuis 1971 à Olivet.

La Hanoïenne n'est pas, à proprement parler, un restaurant. Il serait préférable d'employer à son sujet le terme de « table d'hôte » s'il n'avait pas pris aujourd'hui un sens bien précis.

Vu de l'extérieur, rien ne signale que le pavillon de Monsieur et Madame Nguyen est un restaurant : aucune devanture, aucune enseigne, seule la forme des fers forgés de la grille et du balcon indique que l'endroit est occupé par une famille d'origine asiatique.

Avant d'entrer, il faut sonner pour signaler sa présence comme dans n'importe quelle autre maison de ce lotissement.

Ici les « clients » sont attendus (réservation obligatoire, inutile de venir à l'improviste) et reçus comme des invités.

Lorsque l'on vient manger à la Hanoïenne, on a un peu l'impression de faire partie de la famille Nguyen.

La salle à manger, située au rez-de-chaussée, ne peut accueillir que quatorze convives ce qui renforce le caractère intime de cette formule.

C'est la maîtresse de maison, Madame Kim-Thong Nguyen qui est aux cuisines et qui prépare avec l'aide de ses enfants et de son époux une authentique cuisine vietnamienne.

La famille Nguyen est arrivée en France en 1964.

Auparavant Monsieur Van-Chau Nguyen occupait d'importantes fonctions politiques au Vietnam.

De 1956 à 1962, sous le régime du Président Diem, il était Directeur Général du Polit-Bureau et plus spécialement chargé de la guerre psychologique.

Farouche adversaire des régimes communistes, il était également chef du Parti du Travail Personnaliste.

Lorsque le Président Diem est assassiné par ses généraux, Monsieur Nguyen quitte le Vietnam pour les États-Unis et devient durant une année, Attaché militaire à Washington.

Sa femme s'occupe alors de faire la cuisine pour les repas servis lors des réceptions diplomatiques.

Persuadé que les Américains ne sont pas étrangers à la disparition du Président

Diem, Monsieur Nguyen quitte ce pays pour la France en 1964.

En 1965, il devient professeur d'Histoire à l'École St-Euverte d'Orléans, poste qu'il occupe encore aujourd'hui à soixante ans. Éternel étudiant, Monsieur Nguyen vient, par ailleurs, de s'inscrire à l'Université de Paris VII pour mener à bien un D.E.A.

Mais en 1965, lorsque l'on est réfugié vietnamien et petit professeur d'Histoire, nourrir une famille de neuf enfants n'est pas chose facile tous les jours.

La situation devient encore plus difficile lorsque les aînés débutent leurs études supérieures (les neuf enfants Nguyen vont d'ailleurs suivre ce cursus).

Monsieur et Madame Nguyen décident alors de se lancer dans la restauration, la maîtresse de maison ayant déjà exercé cette activité à Washington.

C'est ainsi que depuis douze ans les Orléanais peuvent déguster une cuisine d'ambassadeur dans un modeste pavillon Olivetain.

Mais l'installation d'un restaurant dans son lieu d'habitation ne va pas sans quelques gymnastiques administratives pour être en règle avec la loi.

C'est ainsi que Monsieur Nguyen est devenu juridiquement l'unique propriétaire

de son pavillon et qu'aux yeux de la loi son épouse n'en est que la locataire : la salle à manger et la cuisine ont été symboliquement séparées en deux, une partie pour le restaurant et l'autre pour la vie familiale.

Monsieur Nguyen garde un souvenir du jour où les contrôleurs de l'administration sont venus mesurer son pavillon sur toutes les coutures, attribuant aux époux Nguyen leur espace respectif.

Si sur le papier les choses ont été compliquées, dans la vie tout se passe dans la plus parfaite harmonie.

Madame Nguyen est aux fourneaux et les autres membres de la famille l'aident lorsque leurs emplois du temps les y autorisent.

En plus des plats traditionnels de la cuisine vietnamienne (souvent baptisée à tort cuisine chinoise) : pâtés impériaux, potages aux parfums d'Asie, canards, poulets, riz cantonnais... Madame Nguyen prépare (à la demande) quatre spécialités de haute tenue : le cochon laqué, le canard désossé farci reconstitué laqué et décoré (une pure merveille), le crabe farçi et une étonnante fondue vietnamienne.

Quant aux prix pratiqués à la Hanoïenne, ils sont très sages comme le sont en général les tarifs des restaurants asiatiques mais celui-ci se distingue par son excellent rapport qualité/prix.

Autant dire qu'il est prudent (et même obligatoire) de réserver sa table pour être l'un des quatorze privilégiés à venir manger à la table de Monsieur et Madame Nguyen.

Signalons également que la Hanoïenne propose des plats cuisinés à emporter et que cette formule connaît un très grand succès.

On vient de loin (Montargis, Étampes, Chartres...) pour pouvoir déguster les spécialités de Madame Nguyen.

Ce succès, qui n'a jamais baissé depuis près de dix ans, n'est dû qu'au bouche à oreille puisque le restaurant la Hanoïenne n'a jamais voulu faire de publicité n'étant pas en mesure de satisfaire un afflux massif de clientèle.

La seule « publicité » dont bénéficie actuellement Monsieur Nguyen on la trouve dans les journaux officiels vietnamiens.

Les nouveaux maîtres du pays continuent à voir dans ce paisible professeur d'Histoire d'Orléans « l'un des plus grands traîtres au pays ».

Une accusation que Monsieur Nguyen tient à rectifier : Traître au parti, sûrement, traître au pays jamais.

The big day arrived, and I remember it very well. We had attached a sign that read "La Hanoïenne" to the entrance with two pieces of string to mark the opening of the family restaurant. There were wooden chairs and repurposed tables, we converted two bedrooms into a dining room, and we even managed to fit customers in the garage.

Ông manned the reception desk, while the boys and I worked in the kitchen and the girls waited the tables.

The specialty of the house was my pan-fried shrimp and my spring rolls, of course. I made them by the thousands. I would often fall asleep in the kitchen late at night after the dinner service. Later, people in the neighborhood called me by the nickname "Madame Spring Roll."

1 pound 2 ounces (500 g) shell-on shrimp (about ¾ ounce/20 g each)

Salt

4 cloves garlic (13 g)

4 teaspoons (20 g) soy sauce

¼ teaspoon (0.5 g) ground black pepper, plus more to taste

1¾ teaspoons (7 g) sugar

5 ounces (150 g) dried rice vermicelli noodles

2 scallions (25 g)

⅔ cup (140 g) sunflower oil

2 to 3 shallots (40 g)

Lettuce leaves

Fresh cilantro

Thai basil

Spring Roll Dipping Sauce (page 211)

FRANCE

Tôm nướng

Preparation time:
40 minutes
Cooking time: 30 minutes
Resting time: 1 hour

TIP
• This dish can also be
served rolled in rice and
tapioca starch wrappers.

PREPARING THE SHRIMP

— Wash the shrimp, adding salt to remove any impurities from the shells. Drain and wipe each shrimp with a clean cloth. Use scissors to cut the shell of a shrimp along its entire length. Then use a knife to split the shell along its entire length without piercing the thin shell covering the belly and clean off any impurities. Repeat with the remaining shrimp. Peel and thinly slice the garlic. In a bowl, combine the shrimp, garlic, soy sauce, pepper, and sugar. Mix and rest for 1 hour.

FOR THE ACCOMPANIMENTS

— Fill a large saucepan with 4¼ cups (1 liter) cold water. Add the noodles and a pinch of salt, and bring to a boil over medium heat. Cook for 5 to 10 minutes. Turn off the heat, cover, and let stand for 5 minutes. Drain, rinse in cold water, and set aside.

Wash and thinly slice the scallions. Heat ⅓ cup (70 g) of the sunflower oil in a saucepan over medium heat, add the scallions, and season with salt. After 5 minutes, stir. As soon as the scallions are colored, remove from the heat and pour half over the noodles. Set aside the other half.

Peel and slice the shallots into thin rings. Heat the remaining ⅓ cup (70 g) of the oil in a saucepan over medium heat and cook the shallots, stirring regularly, for 5 to 10 minutes, until colored light golden. Turn off the heat and drain the shallots, saving the cooking oil. Let stand.

When the shallots have dried and firmed, mince and pour half over the noodles. Set aside the other half.

COOKING AND ASSEMBLY

— Put the shallot cooking oil into a large skillet over high heat. Place the shrimp flesh side down in the pan. After 4 minutes, turn over and cook for another 4 minutes. Drain. Transfer the pan-fried shrimp to a dish. Add the reserved fried scallions and shallots, then season with pepper.

Put a lettuce leaf into a large bowl, then add the noodles. Carefully peel the shrimp and add to the bowl, along with fresh cilantro, Thai basil, and spring roll dipping sauce •.

lòu :

g bàng trừng (t...

bò rát (bò fh...

đường nhuyễn...

ăm :

trừng thật mỏ...

(khoảng 1/4 lượng

chin :

thau trừng đường trên 1 mỏ nước

The house became a great hive of activity. The children worked, played,
            did their homework, washed dishes, set tables, served the
            food, welcomed customers, went to bed late, and got up
            early. In turn, Ông prepared his classes, imposed disci-
            pline at school, treating his students like soldiers, and
            he managed the family, and prayed. And I kept myself busy
            with my cooking.

Money was finally coming in. We were able to send our nine children to
            the best schools in the region—Saint-Charles and Sainte-
            Croix—where they received a strict Catholic education.
            Sainte-Croix was also where Ông received his teaching
            degree. It was an emotional time, too. It coincided with
            the end of the Vietnam War. The country's freedom, one
            man's victory.

In 1984, La Hanoïenne, our family restaurant, was acknowledged with an
            award from *Gault et Millau*. It was a source of pride for
            the family.

It was also the year you were born.

However, all joy is fragile. Some time later, Ông became ill. As often as
            possible, I made him a soup. Bún riêu is a crab soup that
            reminded him of his country.

Crab

1 (about 1¼-pound/600-g) female brown crab

2½-inch (6-cm) piece ginger (100 g)

3 cloves garlic

1 onion (3½ ounces/100 g)

4 tomatoes (1 pound/450 g)

1 stalk lemongrass (60 g)

Meatballs

½ cup (20 g) dried shrimp

1 pound 2 ounces (500 g) pork belly

1 bunch cilantro

2 spring onions

½ small white onion (1 ounce/30 g)

1 teaspoon (5 g) nuoc mam (fish sauce)

1¾ teaspoons (4 g) ground black pepper

1 whole egg

Spicy sauce

1 onion (3½ ounces/100 g)

2 tomatoes (7 ounces/200 g)

3 cloves garlic

1 bird's-eye chile

1 stalk lemongrass (60 g)

1½ tablespoons (20 g) sunflower oil

2 tablespoons (20 g) salted roasted peanuts

½ cup (20 g) dried shrimp

1 teaspoon (5 g) Hanoi-style mam tom (shrimp paste)

1 teaspoon (4 g) sugar

1 teaspoon (5 g) nuoc mam (fish sauce)

1 tablespoon (15 g) rice vinegar

Finishing

1 (13-ounce/375-g) package rice noodles

Salt

10½ cups (2 liters) Chicken Broth (page 213)

Nuoc mam (fish sauce; optional)

Fresh cilantro

Freshly ground black pepper

SERVES 4

Bún riêu

**Preparation time:
50 minutes**
Cooking time: 40 minutes

TIP
• If you like more intense flavor, you can add 1 additional teaspoon mam tom or 1 teaspoon shrimp paste.

FOR THE CRAB

— Poach the crab in 6⅓ cups (1.5 liters) boiling water, without salt, for 10 minutes. Remove the crab and set aside the cooking water. Break open the crab, pick out the meat and coral, and set aside. Also set aside the carcass. Peel and thinly slice the ginger, garlic, and onion and peel the tomatoes. Put the carcass into the crab cooking water, then add the lemongrass, ginger, garlic, onion, and tomatoes. Cook for 25 minutes, then strain the broth through cheesecloth or a fine-mesh strainer. Set aside.

FOR THE MEATBALLS

— Soak the dried shrimp in water for 30 minutes. Drain and chop in a food processor. Use a meat grinder fitted with a fine plate to grind the pork belly. Mix together the reserved crabmeat and chopped shrimp. Mince the cilantro stems and spring onions. Peel and thinly slice the white onion. Add everything to the meat and season with the nuoc mam and pepper. Incorporate the egg into the mixture and adjust the seasoning. Shape into small balls and set aside.

FOR THE SPICY SAUCE

— Peel and cut the onion into small dice. Peel the tomatoes and seed them, reserving the cores. Peel and cut the garlic cloves into quarters. Thinly slice the chile and lemongrass. Heat the sunflower oil in a saucepan. Sweat the onions with the tomatoes. Add the garlic, chile, lemongrass, peanuts, dried shrimp, mam tom, sugar, nuoc mam, and rice vinegar • . Cook over low heat, adding a little water if necessary. As soon as the onions are cooked, transfer to a food processor and blend.

ASSEMBLY

— Fill a large saucepan with 4¼ cups (1 liter) cold water. Add the noodles and a pinch of salt, and bring to a boil over medium heat. Cook for 5 to 10 minutes. Turn off the heat, cover, and let stand for 5 minutes. Drain, rinse in cold water, and set aside. Mix the crab broth with the chicken broth and add the tomato cores. Adjust the seasoning with nuoc mam, if necessary. Heat the broth. Add 4 tablespoons of the spicy sauce, then the meatballs, and cook until the broth comes to a boil. Reduce the heat, skim, and cook for 10 minutes. Fill bowls with noodles, meatballs, and broth. Top with fresh cilantro leaves and a sprinkling of pepper.

Bà thương yêu tất cả
các con và các cháu thân
yêu trong gia đình.

Bà hôn ôm thật chặt
vào lòng Bà.

Bà yêu thương
tất cả các cháu gần xa.

Bà loves you very much, my children and grandchildren, beloved of the family. Bà holds you very dear to her heart. Bà loves all of you, both near and far.

Ông missed the sea very much; his village in central Vietnam called to
him. He thought of his country and wanted to go back one
last time. "Your family is your country," I would tell
him. "It's the most beautiful thing we have created."

Before Ông departed for heaven to join his friend the president, his
brother, my brothers, my mother, my father, and all the
stars we discovered on our way, we were awarded the Medal
of the French Family by the French government. It was
certainly his greatest reward.

Life is about perpetually starting over. My own children, in turn, had
children, and now you are all here.

I closed the restaurant when your grandfather died, but I still cook for
you, to feed you and to raise your spirits. Remember that
cooking is a part of you that you offer to others; cooking
with passion and generosity is our greatest value.

I have become the grandmother to fifteen grandchildren, and I have twelve
great-grandchildren. And you, when will you have yours?

You are "Bà's little darlings."

C'est la vie comme ça! That's what life is all about!

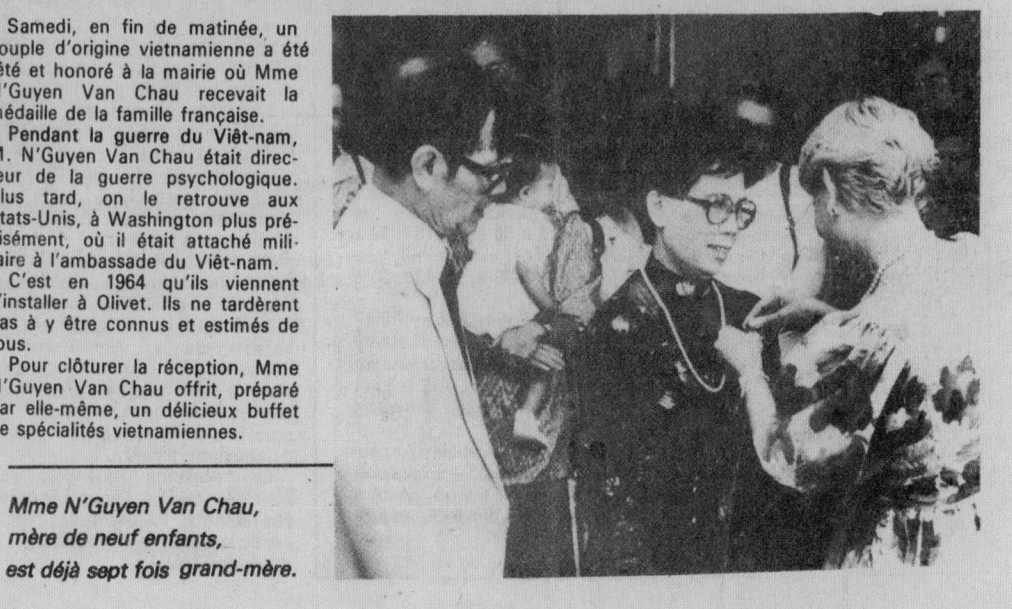

Mme N'Guyen Van Chau reçoit la médaille de la famille française

Samedi, en fin de matinée, un couple d'origine vietnamienne a été fêté et honoré à la mairie où Mme N'Guyen Van Chau recevait la médaille de la famille française.

Pendant la guerre du Viêt-nam, M. N'Guyen Van Chau était directeur de la guerre psychologique. Plus tard, on le retrouve aux Etats-Unis, à Washington plus précisément, où il était attaché militaire à l'ambassade du Viêt-nam.

C'est en 1964 qu'ils viennent s'installer à Olivet. Ils ne tardèrent pas à y être connus et estimés de tous.

Pour clôturer la réception, Mme N'Guyen Van Chau offrit, préparé par elle-même, un délicieux buffet de spécialités vietnamiennes.

Mme N'Guyen Van Chau, mère de neuf enfants, est déjà sept fois grand-mère.

Kids love it!

Thịt băm

SERVES
4

**Preparation time:
20 minutes
Cooking time: 30 minutes**

— Peel and mince the shallots. Heat the sunflower oil in a skillet, sweat the shallots, and add the meat. Cook for 5 to 10 minutes, stirring constantly. Add the nuoc mam, then the caramel syrup, and cook for 20 minutes, or until the liquid reduces and the meat is fried.

Season with the pepper along with minced scallion or cilantro, and adjust the seasoning, if necessary, with nuoc mam or sugar, as desired.

2 shallots (30 g)	¼ cup (60 g) Bà's Caramel Syrup (page 208)
1½ tablespoons (20 g) sunflower oil	¾ teaspoon (2 g) ground black pepper
1 pound 2 ounces (500 g) ground pork shoulder	Scallion or cilantro, minced
2 tablespoons (30 g) nuoc mam (fish sauce), or more to taste	A little sugar (optional)

This hybrid dish is a Vietnamese version of the French steak frites (steak and thin fries).

Thịt bò xào khoai tây

SERVES 4

FRANCE

Preparation time: 40 minutes

Cooking time: 50 minutes

Resting time: 10 minutes

---

4 Yukon Gold potatoes (1¼ pounds/600 g)

Sunflower oil for deep-frying

1¼ pounds (600 g) sirloin or rib steak

Pinch of salt (1 g)

1½ tablespoons (20 g) sunflower oil

---

1 small white onion (2 ounces/60 g)

---

4 cloves garlic

---

4 teaspoons (20 g) nuoc mam (fish sauce)

---

1 tablespoon (18 g) Maggi sauce

Freshly ground black pepper

Scallion (optional)

— Peel and cut the potatoes into 1/16-inch (2-mm)-thick slices. Heat the frying oil to 285°F (140°C) in a saucepan and fry the potatoes until light golden. Watch closely as they cook to prevent them from sticking together. Remove from the oil, drain, and let stand for 10 minutes.

Increase the temperature of the oil to 350°F (180°C) and deep-fry the potatoes again. When golden and crispy, remove, drain, and set aside.

— Season the meat with half of the salt on each side. In a skillet, sear the meat on each side with half of the salt in sunflower oil over high heat. Rest for 20 minutes, then thinly slice.

— Peel and mince the onion. Peel and crush the garlic with a mortar and pestle. In a deep skillet, sauté the meat with the potatoes and onion, then add the crushed garlic, nuoc mam, and Maggi sauce. Season with pepper. Add some chopped scallion, if desired.

Bánh rán

Mung bean filling

1¼ cups (240 g) mung beans

⅓ cup plus 1 tablespoon (80 g) granulated sugar

½ teaspoon (3 g) salt

2 teaspoons (8 g) vanilla sugar

1 cup (80 g) shredded coconut

1½ tablespoons (20 g) sunflower oil

Dough

2 potatoes (8 ounces/220 g)

2½ cups (400 g) glutinous rice flour

⅓ cup (40 g) cornmeal

⅞ cup (180 g) granulated sugar

1 teaspoon (5 g) salt

2 teaspoons (8 g) vanilla sugar

2 tablespoons (30 g) sunflower oil plus more for frying

2¼ teaspoons (8 g) active dry yeast

1⅓ cups (200 g) white sesame seeds

As a child, you used to come into the kitchen with your mother. You were already asking me for this recipe!

Preparation time: 30 minutes

Cooking time: 30 minutes

Resting time: 1 hour

MAKES
20
BALLS

FOR THE MUNG BEAN FILLING

— Rinse the beans. Put them into a saucepan and cover with water. Place the pan over medium heat and cook for 15 to 20 minutes, stirring from time to time. When it comes to a boil, reduce the heat to low and let cook for 20 minutes. Drain the beans when they are soft. Use a ricer or spoon to crush the beans. Add the granulated sugar, salt, vanilla sugar, shredded coconut, and sunflower oil. Mix thoroughly, return to the pan, and cook over very low heat for 5 to 8 minutes, keeping a close watch. Remove from the heat and let cool. Shape into 1¼-inch (3-cm)-diameter balls, each about ½ ounce (16 g), and set aside in a cool place.

FOR THE DOUGH

— Boil the potatoes for 15 to 20 minutes, then let cool. Use a ricer or fork to mash the potatoes and put into a bowl. Add the flour, cornmeal, granulated sugar, salt, vanilla sugar, and oil and mix. Pour in ½ cup (120 ml) warm water at 95°F (35°C) and mix again. Add the yeast, then gradually add 1 cup (240 ml) room temperature water, mixing to a smooth dough that does not stick to your fingers. Depending on the flour and cornmeal and their freshness, you may need more or less water. Knead for 10 to 15 minutes, until the dough is soft and does not stick to your fingers. Put into a container and cover with plastic wrap. Refrigerate for 1 hour.

MAKING THE BALLS

— Remove the dough and mung bean balls from the refrigerator and bring to room temperature. Shape the dough into 1¼-inch (3-cm)-diameter balls, each about 1 ounce (25 g), then roll out into 2½ to 3¼-inch (6 to 8-cm)-diameter disks. Place a bean ball on each disk and bring up the edges of the dough to completely wrap the filling • . Roll the balls in the palms of your hands until perfectly round. Put the sesame seeds onto a plate and roll each ball in the seeds to completely coat, then roll again until perfectly round.

COOKING THE BALLS

— Heat oil in a saucepan to 300°F (150°C). Drop in no more than five or six balls at a time. They must have room to roll around for even cooking. Use a skimmer to gently swirl the balls in the oil. The oil temperature should not exceed 350°F (180°C). After 12 to 15 minutes, the balls will be golden and crispy. Remove, drain, and let stand for a few minutes. Enjoy them crisp and slightly warm.

TIP

• Make sure the balls are fully encased in the dough; otherwise, they may break open when fried.

My dear Bà,

Thank you for these very profound words, for your moving and meaningful testimony. The complexity of your story has long reflected the enigma of my own story and of my Vietnamese background. For a long time, this silence had built up a barrier of unspoken words, the result of cultural voids, making it impossible to express myself freely. Thanks to our time spent cooking together, today your words are heard, and they set mine free. Each dish linked to the story of your exile is one more step toward finding my own story.

Often throughout this story, you wondered why I spent so much time asking you these questions, and one day you told me, "a child duck and a mother chicken can never understand each other." You explained to me in your words, and in your own way, that we each had our own point of view on history, and that there was not just a single truth to be found. Along this journey of initiation, I took up cooking, first out of necessity and later out of pleasure. Little by little, as if by magic, your recipes have come to life in me and given birth to this book.

The following recipes are hybrid recipes, Eurasian like me. They are the result of combining the essentials of your cuisine with cooking techniques and local French products.

As I was learning to cook, I met Roland Theimer, whom you called "Ola," a young and impassioned chef who fell in love with your recipes. We cooked together in a small clandestine workshop in a Parisian restaurant near the Louvre, Maison Maison. We developed Franco-Vietnamese dishes: Vietnamese-style beef bourguignon, tuna tataki with nuoc mam sauce, and chicken salad with rau ram and all the intensity of this peppermint-flavored herb. This laboratory for the exchange of cultures led to a decisive encounter, a meeting with Alain Ducasse, who first published this book in France and to whom I offer my deepest appreciation for his faith, his courage, and his curiosity.

This never-ending story is timeless. I hope that it will be the essence of the story of your exile, that it will inspire our future generations to know where they come from: from the rice paddies of Van Noi near Hanoi, where you ate phở with your father in the morning while crossing the mud puddle in front of the house to the millions of spring rolls you cooked on the stove in your kitchen in France. It is the perpetual renewal of a cuisine that is alive, shared, and, above all, eaten and loved!

Anne-Solenne, Hong Hoa

**Preparation time:
25 minutes**

1 red chile (4 g)

1 tablespoon (16 g) nuoc mam
(fish sauce)

3½ tablespoons (50 g) lime juice

2½ tablespoons (30 g) sugar

3 tablespoons (40 g)
sunflower oil

½ banana blossom
(7 ounces/200 g)

1 lemon

1 sprig of dill

2 passion fruits

1 cup (100 g) bean sprouts

⅓ red onion (1½ ounces/40 g)

Kale shoots (optional)

1 garlic scape (10 g)

¼ cup (40 g) crushed peanuts
(or Fried Shallots, page 212)

Tia to (Vietnamese perilla)
leaves

— Mince the chile. In a bowl, mix the chile with the nuoc mam, lime juice, sugar, and sunflower oil.

— Remove the outer leaves from the banana blossom and discard the undeveloped banana. Slice the heart and quickly drizzle with lemon juice to prevent it from oxidizing. Shred finely and mix with the sauce.

— Mince the dill. Peel and thinly slice the onion. Add the minced dill, passion fruit pulp, bean sprouts, onion, and kale shoots, if using, to the salad and mix. Thinly slice the garlic scape. Sprinkle the crushed peanuts, tia to leaves, and garlic scape over the salad. Serve quickly, before the banana blossom oxidizes.

SERVES
4

FRANCE

Nộm hoa
chuối

SERVES
6

Broth

1 onion (3½ ounces/100 g)

2-inch (6-cm) piece ginger
(100 g)

10 cloves garlic

2 stalks lemongrass

¾ cup (180 g) nuoc mam
(fish sauce)

4 chicken legs

5 teaspoons (10 g) lemon zest

Base

1-inch (2.5-cm) piece ginger
(40 g)

⅔ stalk lemongrass (40 g)

¼ cup (60 g) sunflower oil

2 tablespoons (30 g) nuoc mam
(fish sauce)

⅔ lime (40 g)

6 to 8 scallions (100 g)

40 to 50 rau ram
(Vietnamese cilantro)
leaves (20 g)

Black sesame seeds

Gỏi gà xé phay

**Preparation time:
30 minutes
Cooking time:
20 to 30 minutes**

FOR THE BROTH

— Peel and cut the onion into quarters. Peel the ginger and garlic. Mince the lemongrass. Put 3¼ quarts (3 liters) water into a large pot with the lemongrass, onions, ginger, garlic, and nuoc mam. Add the chicken legs, then place over the heat. When the broth reaches 195°F (90°C), remove from the heat, cover with a lid, and let cook with the residual heat for 15 minutes, adding the lemon zest after 10 minutes.

FOR THE BASE

— While the broth is cooking, prepare the base. Peel and finely chop the ginger, mince the lemongrass, then mix the ginger, lemongrass, sunflower oil, nuoc mam, and juice from the lime.

ASSEMBLY

— When the broth is cooked, remove the chicken and let cool. Debone and thinly slice the meat. Add the chicken meat to the base and mix. Slice the scallions. Mix with the base. At the last minute, wash and pluck the rau ram leaves and add • . Sprinkle with black sesame seeds and serve immediately.

TIP
• Add the rau ram at the last minute because the leaves wilt very quickly.

Cá ngừ tataki

![Tuna tataki dish in a bowl]

1¼ pounds (600 g) center-cut tuna fillet (bluefin, yellowfin, or albacore)

Pinch of salt (1 g)

3 tablespoons (40 g) sunflower oil

4 teaspoons (20 g) soy sauce

½-inch (1-cm) piece young ginger (20 g)

½ cup (20 g) finely minced cilantro

¼ green garlic (young garlic plant), leaves and flowers only (10 g)

2 spring onions, greens only (40 g)

A few small pieces of habanero chile (optional)

Sauce

1 teaspoon (4 g) sesame oil

3½ tablespoons (50 g) lime juice

3 tablespoons (40 g) sunflower oil

5 teaspoons (24 g) nuoc mam (fish sauce)

2 cloves garlic (6 g)

SERVES 4

Preparation time:
10 minutes
Resting time: 20 minutes

TIPS
• Habanero chile is very hot. Use with caution.
•• To enhance the flavor of this dish, you can also top with fried shallots (page 212).

PREPARING THE TUNA

— Season the fish with the salt, rubbing well on each side. Sear on one side in a skillet with the sunflower oil. Glaze with the soy sauce. Remove the tuna from the heat and refrigerate for 10 minutes to cool a little.

FOR THE SAUCE

— Mix together the sesame oil, lime juice, sunflower oil, and nuoc mam. Peel and crush the garlic cloves, then add to the sauce.

FINISHING

— Peel and finely mince the young ginger. Finely mince the herbs and thinly slice the spring onion greens on the diagonal. Mix everything with the sauce. Add the chile, if using •.

When the tuna has cooled down, cut into ¾ by 1¼-inch (2 x 3-cm) triangular pieces. Cover the tuna with sauce 1 minute before serving ••.

Trai xào

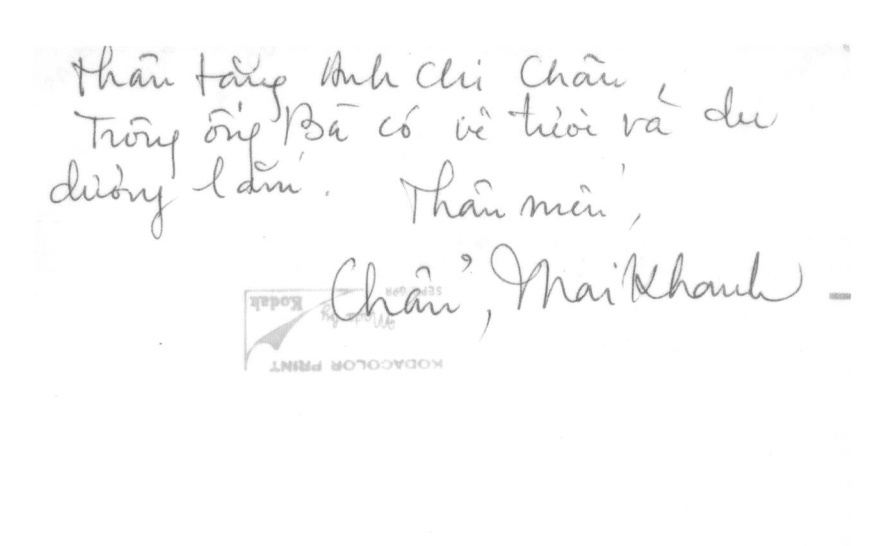

Preparation time:
5 minutes
Cooking time: 4 minutes

TIP
• You can also use
this recipe to prepare
scallops on a grill,
adding the condiments
directly to the
previously opened shell.

— Thinly slice the lemongrass and scallions. Peel and mince the garlic. Heat the sunflower oil in a skillet and sauté the lemongrass for 30 seconds. Add the clams, spring onions, garlic, rice water, and nuoc mam. Cover with a lid and cook until the clams open • .

— Serve the clams with the sliced scallions, seasoning with lime juice, if desired.

⅔ stalk lemongrass (40 g)

4 scallions (about 2 ounces/60 g)

4 cloves garlic

3 tablespoons (40 g)
sunflower oil

48 clams (12 clams per person)

1 cup (150 g) thinly sliced
spring onions

1⅓ cups (320 g) unsalted rice
water or rice wine

2½ tablespoons (40 g)
nuoc mam (fish sauce)

Juice of ½ lime (optional)

SERVES
4

Atiso

SERVES 4

**Preparation time:
30 minutes
Cooking time: 10 minutes**

Juice of 1 lemon

6 poivrage (small) artichokes

2 large spring onions (70 g)

2 cloves garlic (6 g)

1 tablespoon (16 g) nuoc mam
(fish sauce)

2½ teaspoons (12 g) lemon juice,
plus 1 teaspoon (2 g) lemon zest,
or more to taste

2 bird's-eye chiles

3 tablespoons (40 g)
sunflower oil

¾ teaspoon (2 g) ground black
pepper

3 tablespoons (10 g) minced dill

— Squeeze the juice of one lemon into a bowl. Remove the leaves from the artichokes, cut lengthwise into quarters, and remove the choke, if necessary. Immediately put into the bowl of lemon juice, tossing to coat, to keep them from turning dark.

— Cut the spring onions into quarters. Peel and finely mince the garlic. Mix it with the nuoc mam, the 2½ teaspoons (12 g) lemon juice, and the lemon zest.

— Mince the chiles. Sauté the artichokes and spring onions in the sunflower oil over high heat for 6 to 10 minutes, until golden brown. Add the pepper and chiles 1 minute before the end of cooking, then drain off the excess oil, if necessary, and deglaze the pan with the garlic–nuoc mam–lemon mixture. Serve with dill.

1¼ pounds (600 g) lean beef

2 cloves garlic (6 g)

½-inch (1-cm) piece young ginger (20 g)

1 teaspoon (4 g) toasted sesame oil

2½ tablespoons (40 g) nuoc mam (fish sauce)

2½ tablespoons (40 g) lime juice

1 teaspoon (4 g) sugar

2 spring onions (60 g)

½ teaspoon (1 g) lemon zest

Cilantro or Thai basil shoots

SERVES 4

Thịt bò sống tái

FRANCE

Preparation time: 10 minutes

TIP
• When serving raw meat, it is best to buy it from your neighborhood butcher to get the freshest, most tender meat available.

— Use a knife to finely chop the meat and set aside in the refrigerator. Make the sauce: Peel and mince the garlic and young ginger. Mix the sesame oil with the nuoc mam, lime juice, sugar, garlic, and ginger. Slice the spring onions on the diagonal. Pour the sauce over the meat immediately before serving, and garnish with spring onions, lemon zest, and cilantro or Thai basil shoots •.

2 ounces (60 g) dried
cellophane noodles

1½ ounces (40 g) wood ear
mushrooms

Sunflower oil

3½ ounces (100 g) firm tofu

2 cloves garlic (6 g)

2½ tablespoons (40 g) lime juice

4 teaspoons (20 g) nuoc mam
(fish sauce)

2½ tablespoons (30 g) sugar

1 to 2 shallots (30 g)

2 small red bell peppers
(5 ounces/140 g)

8 cilantro leaves, finely minced

8 rau ram (Vietnamese cilantro)
leaves, finely minced

Pinch of ground black pepper
(1 g)

SERVES 4

**Preparation time:
20 minutes
Cooking time: 20 minutes
Resting time: 50 minutes**

FOR THE NOODLES AND TOFU

— Soak the noodles in hot water for 15 minutes, or drop into boiling salted water for 1 to 2 minutes. Drain and set aside. Soak the mushrooms in hot water for 15 to 20 minutes, until soft.

Heat ½ inch (1 cm) of sunflower oil in a saucepan. Cut the tofu into cubes. When the oil is hot, add the tofu and turn it over frequently to color on all sides. Remove from the pan, drain, and set aside.

FOR THE SAUCE

— Peel and crush the garlic in a mortar and pestle. Put into a bowl and mix with the lime juice, nuoc mam, sugar, and 3 tablespoons (40 g) sunflower oil.

ASSEMBLY

— Slice the mushrooms. Peel and cut the shallots into rings. Finely chop the bell peppers. Mix the noodles with the mushrooms, shallots, bell pepper, and fried tofu, and put onto plates. Pour over the sauce, then sprinkle each serving with one or two cilantro and rau ram leaves. Add the ground pepper.

Bún tàu

FRANCE

Thịt bò kho

**Preparation time:
25 minutes
Cooking time: 3 hours**

1½ pounds (700 g) chuck steak, tendons not removed

4 onions (14 ounces/400 g)

2 (3½-ounce/100-g) disks palm sugar

2 bird's-eye chiles, seeded

6 whole cloves garlic (20 g)

1½ tablespoons (10 g) freshly ground green pepper

4-inch (10-cm) piece ginger (150 g)

10 green cardamom pods

1¼ teaspoons (2 g) coriander seeds

2 whole star anise

2 stalks lemongrass

2 Vietnamese cinnamon sticks

2 tablespoons (30 g) nuoc mam (fish sauce)

¾ cup (180 g) soy sauce

— Cut the meat into 1½-inch (4-cm) cubes. Peel and coarsely mince the onions. Heat the palm sugar disks in a stainless steel saucepan. When the sugar is melted and a light brown color, add the meat to brown.

— When the meat is golden, add the onions and sauté until golden. Reduce the heat and cook over low heat. Add the chile, garlic, and pepper. Peel and cut the ginger into ¾-inch (2-cm) cubes and add to the pan. Put the cardamom, coriander seeds, star anise, lemongrass, and cinnamon sticks into a spice bag, close tightly, and add to the pan. Add the nuoc mam, soy sauce, and 1⅔ cups (400 g) water. Cover with a lid and cook for 3 hours, until the meat is soft and brown. Serve with rice.

SERVES 4

14 ounces (400 g) round steak

¼ teaspoon (2 g) salt

¼ cup (60 g) sunflower oil

6 cloves garlic (20 g)

¼ red onion (1 ounce/30 g)

4 teaspoons (20 g) nuoc mam (fish sauce)

2 red chiles

Juice of 2 limes

2 medlars

1 star fruit (carambola; 2 ounces/120 g)

1 cup (5 ounces/140 g) cherry tomatoes

Mint leaves

Garlic shoots

SERVES 4

Gỏi bò khế

F R
A N
C E

Preparation time:
10 minutes
Cooking time: 5 minutes
Resting time: 20 minutes

— Rub the meat with the salt. Heat 1½ tablespoons (20 g) of the sunflower oil in a skillet over high heat. Sear the meat, keeping it rare or even raw inside. Remove from the heat and rest for 20 minutes.

— Cut the meat into thin slices. Peel and grate the garlic with a Microplane, or finely mince. Peel and thinly slice the red onion. Seed and finely chop the red chiles. Mix the meat with the garlic and onion, then add the nuoc mam, the remaining sunflower oil, and the chile.

— Squeeze the juice from the limes into a bowl. Peel the medlars and coat them with the lime juice to prevent them from oxidizing. Cut into slices and then small dice, and put into the bowl with the juice. Slice the star fruit and cut the cherry tomatoes into quarters. Add the diced medlar, star fruit slices, and cherry tomato quarters to the meat mixture and mix gently. Mince the mint and garlic shoots. Add to the mixture. Adjust the seasoning with a dash of nuoc mam or lime juice, if necessary.

2 cups (400 g) soybeans
(preferably small, round,
and a light color)

4 to 6 pandan leaves (25 g)

1¼ cups (250 g) sugar

1 teaspoon (6 g) salt

FRANCE

SERVES 15

Sữa đậu nành

**Preparation time:
30 minutes
Cooking time: 50 minutes
Resting time: 10 hours**

— A day in advance, rinse the soybeans three times. Soak in 2 cups (500 ml) water for 10 hours, keeping them totally immersed.

— Use a blender to blend the beans with a little soaking water in four 9-ounce (250-g) batches. Strain the contents of the blender through a strainer lined with a clean, damp cloth, which in turn is placed over a stockpot with a capacity of at least 5 quarts (5 liters) to collect the milk. Gather the corners of the cloth together to make a ball and hold tightly while squeezing to extract as much milk as possible. Repeat the process as many times as necessary, then discard the pulp once all the milk has been extracted. Add more water as needed to yield 3¾ quarts (3.5 liters) of liquid. Place the pot over low heat for 20 minutes, stirring regularly to avoid sediment formation at the bottom of the pot that could burn.

— Wash the pandan leaves and trim off the ends. Use one leaf to tie all the others into a bunch. Put into the pot and cook for 20 minutes. As soon as the milk comes to a boil, take out the leaves and reduce the heat. Stir in the sugar and salt and cook for another 10 minutes. Turn off the heat and let cool. Transfer to a bottle and refrigerate • .

TIP
• This vitamin-packed drink can be enjoyed hot or cold, sweetened or unsweetened. It will keep in the refrigerator for three to four days.

APPENDICES

APPENDICES

APPENDICES

APPENDICES

APPENDICES

SAUCES

Spicy Lemon Sauce

Makes about ⅓ cup (80 g)
Preparation time: 10 minutes

1 red chile (4 g)

3 cloves garlic (8 g)

1½ tablespoons (20 g) sugar

2 teaspoons (10 g) nuoc mam (fish sauce)

1 tablespoon (15 g) lime juice

— Cut the chile into pieces. Peel and degerm the garlic. Put the sugar, chile, and garlic into a mortar. Use the pestle to crush the ingredients while mixing. Gradually add the nuoc mam, then the lime juice. Add 4 teaspoons (7 g) water heated to 70°F (20°C) and mix well. Adjust the seasoning to taste.

TIP • This sauce goes well with broiled or steamed fish dishes.

Pineapple and Anchovy Sauce

Serves 4
Preparation time: 10 minutes
Cooking time: 10 minutes

2 cloves garlic (6 g)

1 shallot (20 g)

²/₃ cup (3½ ounces/100 g) finely chopped pineapple

5 teaspoons (25 g) mam nem (anchovy dipping sauce) or 50 g anchovies in oil

2 teaspoons (10 g) sunflower oil

2½ teaspoons (10 g) sugar

Nuoc mam (fish sauce; optional)

2 teaspoons (10 g) lime juice

— Peel and grate the garlic. Peel and thinly slice the shallot. Mix the pineapple, garlic, shallot, mam nem, sunflower oil, sugar, and 3½ tablespoons (50 g) water in a saucepan.

Cover with a lid and cook over low heat for about 10 minutes. Adjust the seasoning with nuoc mam, if necessary. Let cool, then serve with the lime juice.

TIP • This sauce goes well with boiled meat.

Ginger Sauce

Serves 4
Preparation time: 10 minutes
Resting time: 10 to 15 minutes

1¼-inch (3-cm) piece young ginger (50 g)

3 cloves garlic (preferably new garlic)

1 red chile (4 g; optional)

5 teaspoons (25 g) nuoc mam (fish sauce)

1½ tablespoons (25 g) lime juice

2½ teaspoons (10 g) sugar

— Peel and mince the ginger. Peel and finely mince the garlic. If adding the chile, seed and cut into small pieces. Mix the ginger with the garlic, nuoc mam, lime juice, sugar, and chile, if using. Let stand for 10 to 15 minutes before use.

Bà's Caramel Syrup

Makes about ⅓ cup (100 g)
Preparation time: 5 minutes
Cooking time: 10 minutes

½ cup (100 g) sugar

— Combine the sugar and 2 tablespoons plus 2 teaspoons (40 g) water in a saucepan and cook over medium heat while watching closely. Stir lightly at first, then do not stir again. Cook for 10 minutes. As soon as the caramel turns a dark brown color and gives off a fairly strong smell, remove from the heat.

Stir in ¾ cup plus 1 tablespoon (200 g) water (be very careful, because it may splatter) to keep the caramel syrup for longer. You can store it for one week in a jar at room temperature.

Spring Roll Dipping Sauce

Serves 4
Preparation time: 5 minutes

2 cloves garlic (6 g)

1½ tablespoons (20 g) sugar

3½ tablespoons (50 g) nuoc mam (fish sauce)

2 tablespoons (30 g) rice vinegar or lime juice

— Peel and mince the garlic. Heat ⅓ cup plus 1½ tablespoons (100 g) water, add the sugar, and wait for the mixture to cool. Mix in the nuoc mam, vinegar, and minced garlic.

Tamarind Sauce

Serves 4
Preparation time: 10 minutes
Cooking time: 5 minutes

3 onions (10½ ounces/300 g)

1½ tablespoons (20 g) sunflower oil

2 teaspoons (10 g) soy sauce

1½-inch (4-cm) piece ginger (60 g)

1½ tablespoons (20 g) sugar

2½ tablespoons (40 g) tamarind paste

1 teaspoon (4 g) nuoc mam (fish sauce), or more to taste

— Peel and thinly slice the onions. Sauté in a saucepan with the sunflower oil. When cooked, deglaze the pan with the soy sauce. Peel and thinly slice the ginger. Heat 1 cup (240 g) water in a saucepan with the ginger, sugar, and tamarind paste. Work the paste with a wooden spoon to dissolve. When the liquid turns brown and thickens, after about 5 minutes, strain through a fine-mesh strainer. Adjust the seasoning with nuoc mam. Add the cooked onions and mix with the tamarind sauce.

Mango Sauce

Makes about 1 cup (160 g)
Preparation time: 12 minutes

1 shallot (20 g)

1 bird's-eye chile

1 clove garlic (3 g)

⅔ cup (100 g) finely chopped ripe mango

¼ teaspoon (1 g) sugar

⅓ teaspoon (2 g) salt

4 teaspoons (20 g) lime juice

1 tablespoon (15 g) nuoc mam (fish sauce)

— Peel and finely mince the shallot. Seed and finely chop the chile. Peel and grate the garlic with a Microplane grater. Mix the mango with the shallot, chile, and garlic in a bowl. Season with the sugar, salt, lime juice, and nuoc mam.

BASIC RECIPES

Fried Shallots

Makes about 3 cups (160 g)
Preparation time: 15 minutes
Cooking time: 10 minutes

20 to 25 shallots (400 g)

4¼ cups (1 liter) sunflower oil

— Peel and thinly slice the shallots. Put the sunflower oil into a saucepan and add the shallots. Put the pan over the heat and fry the shallots for about 10 minutes, until lightly colored, not dark. Remove the pan from the heat. The shallots will continue to cook off the heat. Drain the fried shallots, saving the cooking oil.

TIP • Use the shallot-infused oil to make other dishes.

Bánh Cuòn Dipping Sauce

Preparation time: 5 minutes

2 cloves garlic (6 g)

⅓ cup plus 1½ tablespoons (100 g) lime juice

3½ tablespoons (50 g) nuoc mam (fish sauce)

— Peel and thinly slice the garlic. Mix the lime juice with the nuoc mam and add the garlic.

Prawn Bisque

Makes ¾ cup (200 g)
Preparation time: 25 minutes
Cooking time: 15 minutes

4 onions (14 ounces/400 g)

2¼-inch (7-cm) piece ginger (100 g)

6 cloves garlic (18 g)

3 tomatoes (10½ ounces/300 g)

Heads and shells of 7 ounces (200 g) large shrimp

2 tablespoons (30 g) sunflower oil

4 stalks lemongrass

2 tablespoons (30 g) rice vinegar

2 tablespoons (30 g) nuoc mam (fish sauce)

— Peel and coarsely chop the onions, ginger, and garlic. Chop the tomatoes. Brown all the shrimp heads and shells in a large stockpot with the sunflower oil. Add the onions, ginger, garlic, tomatoes, and lemongrass. Sauté over high heat for 5 minutes. When the contents of the pan are golden brown, use a wooden spoon to break up the heads, and deglaze the pan with the rice vinegar. Add the nuoc mam and 1 cup plus 1½ tablespoons (260 g) water, cover with a lid, and cook over medium for 10 minutes. Strain the bisque through a fine-mesh strainer.

Annatto Oil

Makes 2 teaspoons (10 g)
Cooking time: 5 to 10 minutes

1 tablespoon (10 g) annatto seeds

2 teaspoons (10 g) sunflower oil

— Put the sunflower oil into a small saucepan over low heat. Add the annatto seeds. Stir frequently for 5 to 10 minutes. When the oil starts to bubble and turn red, strain and let cool.

Shrimp Bisque

Makes 1¼ cup (300 g)
Preparation time: 30 minutes
Cooking time: 15 minutes

Heads and shells of 1 pound 2 ounces (600 g) small shrimp

½ cup (100 g) sugar

4 teaspoons (20 g) rice vinegar

4 teaspoons (20 g) nuoc mam (fish sauce)

— Put the shrimp heads and shells into a saucepan with 1⅔ cups (400 ml) water, the sugar, vinegar, and nuoc mam. Simmer over low heat for 10 minutes. Let cool and strain.

Chicken Broth

Makes 10½ cups
Preparation time: 15 minutes
Cooking time: 1 hour 30 minutes

1 stew hen

3¼ quarts (3 liters) cold water

⅔ cup (150 g) nuoc mam (fish sauce)

— Wash and dry the hen well, then remove the giblets. Use a chef's torch to singe the skin for 5 minutes. Pour 3¼ quarts (3 liters) cold water into a stockpot and put the hen inside, making sure it is totally submerged. Bring to a simmer, skim off the scum, then add the nuoc mam. Cover with a lid and simmer over low heat for 1 hour 30 minutes. Remove the hen and reserve for other uses. Strain the broth to remove all impurities.

TIP • For a more intensely flavored broth, you can add 3 stalks lemongrass and a ¾-inch (2-cm) piece of ginger (30 g) at the end and simmer the broth for 20 more minutes.

Lemon Dipping Sauce

Makes about 2 teaspoons
Prep time: 2 minutes

1 heaping teaspoon fine salt

1 teaspoon ground black pepper

Juice of 1 lemon

— Combine the salt and pepper in a ramekin. Mix in the lemon juice.

Diners are served individual servings of the sauce to dip their chicken into throughout the meal.

CONTENTS

RECIPE INDEX

INGREDIENT INDEX

MY THANKS

To Alain Ducasse, for having faith in me, for supporting my efforts, and, consequently, for allowing Bà's way of cooking to gain the recognition it deserves.

To Rizzoli, for honoring Bà's cuisine and heritage throughout the world. A special thanks to Stéphanie Bardon, and to John Ripoll and Theresa Bebbington for the English translation.

To Romain Meder and his whole team for giving me such a royal welcome at the Plaza Athénée.

To Aurore Charoy, director of Éditions Ducasse, for immediately supporting my project and encouraging me to believe in it. To Pierre Tachon, art director at Soins Graphiques, for his watchful eye and valuable advice.

To Bà, my beloved grandmother, for those unforgettable moments when you shared your wisdom with me and for giving me your unconditional love.

To Chu Tung, my uncle whom I love and without whom I could not have written this book. Dear to Bà and the whole family, this talented chef ensured that lessons were learned, supervised the production of the dishes, and developed the traditional recipes of the family in this book with precision and taste.

To Roland Theimer, who gave me the opportunity to learn from him, for his patience and great talent.

To Jessica Rostain, the editor of this book, for her professionalism and sensitivity, and also all of her team, Margaux and Laila, for their efforts.

To the team at Soins Graphiques for the beautiful layout of this book, and especially to Aurélie Mansion for her talent and ideas. My thanks also go to Liana Korios.

To David Sochanek, for his constant support, friendship, and participation in the book.

To Pierre Monetta, for his creative eye and great sense of humor.

To the entire team at Zenchef for allowing us to produce this book and to share Bà's little culinary secrets.

AND ALSO...

To my mother, Loan Hatte, the guardian of all these dishes, who has been present at every stage of my life with love and support.

To my father, Xavier Hatte, the son of my grandfather, both exceptional French cooks, for allowing me to educate my palate and to love the local produce grown and reared by French farmers.

To my sister Victoria, my sister Juliette, and my brother Robin, and their three mixed-race, Franco-Vietnamese and Franco-Guyanese children, for their melding of cultures and zest for life.

To Coyen (Kim Yen Sartorius), my mother's twin sister, for introducing me to healthy Vietnamese cuisine and traditional Chinese medicine and for her unfailing support.

To all my family, to Ông and Bà, to Bac Long, Bac Lân, Bac Quy, Co Phượng, Chu Tài, Chu Lộc, to Chu Ninh, Co Phượng, Chu Truong, Co Thuy—their children and grandchildren—and to all my cousins. Special thanks in particular to Binh—my beloved cousin—and to Quentin, Jade and Max Sartorius, Lan Nguyen, Tai Nguyen, Nathalie Lucas-Verdier, Audrey Nguyen, Mayu Yamasaki, Minh, and Cha Anh for the part they played in the making of this book.

To Aimée Buidine, my producer, coauthor, and friend, with whom we are now preparing Saveurs d'exil (Flavors of Exile), a documentary film about my Vietnamese family's experiences during the Indochina War and Vietnam War and the period covered in this book; and to Julien Madon, her business partner.

To Quiet, especially to Sol Guy and his fantastic team, for truly caring about the empowerment of artists.

To La Belle Mine, a Parisian bistro serving natural wines in the city's 5th arrondissement, and especially to Thomas, Yan, Yannick, and Juliet, who encouraged me to cook and inspired me to start a business.

To Hubert d'Artemare, for his unending support; to Jean-François Hubert and Boi Tran, for their guidance on Vietnamese culture, and for making me aware of the kingdom of Champa and the culinary delights of Huế; to Mr. and Mrs. Pham for their great support; to Delphine Ghosarossian—"Madame Photo"; to Nick Ut, Peter Arnett, Professor Thầy Kiệt, and Thao Griffith for their invaluable knowledge on the Vietnam War; to Neung and Alexis de Rendinger, Nick Mathers, Minh Tran Dinh, Marie-Pierre Dillenseger and Xavier Zeitoun for their indispensable help in preparing this book.

To the future generation—and especially my own future child—to all my and Bà's friends, for their precious support, and to you, dear readers and future ambassadors for Bà's cuisine.

Collection Director
Alain Ducasse

Director
Aurore Charoy

Editor
Jessica Rostain
Gloria Nantz for the English edition

Photography
Pierre Monetta
page 5 and back cover, left top: © Nam Quan
page 120: © Anne-Solenne Hatte
page 121: © David Sochanek
page 218: © Flavio Manriquez and Timothée Alazraki

Art Direction and Graphic Design
Soins Graphiques
*Pierre Tachon, Aurélie Mansion, Camille Demaimay,
and Liana Korios*

Cover design for the English edition
Kayleigh Jankowski

Photoengraving
Nord Compo

English translation and copyediting
John Ripoll and Theresa Bebbington for Cillero
& de Motta

The editor warmly thanks Sophie Dupuis-Gaulier for her
patience and professionalism.
Many thanks to Keyza Romil for her invaluable assistance.
Many thanks to Rebecca Genet for the styling of the beautiful
bowl on the cover.

First published in the United States of America in 2021 by
Rizzoli International Publications, Inc.
300 Park Avenue South
New York, NY 10010
www.rizzoliusa.com

Originally published in French in 2019 as
La Cuisine de Bà
by Ducasse Edition
© 2019 Ducasse Edition

Printed in China
2021 2022 2023 2024 / 10 9 8 7 6 5 4 3 2 1
ISBN: 978-0-8478-6918-3
Library of Congress Control Number: 2021934379

Visit us online:
Facebook.com/RizzoliNewYork
Twitter: @Rizzoli_Books
Instagram.com/RizzoliBooks
Pinterest.com/RizzoliBooks
Youtube.com/user/RizzoliNY
Issuu.com/Rizzoli